GloboChrist

THE CHURCH
AND POSTMODERN
CULTURE

James K. A. Smith, series editor
www.churchandpomo.org

The Church and Postmodern
Culture series features high-profile
theorists in continental philosophy
and contemporary theology
writing for a broad, nonspecialist
audience interested in the impact of
postmodern theory on the faith and
practice of the church.

Also available in the series

James K. A. Smith, *Who's Afraid of Postmodernism? Taking Derrida, Lyotard, and Foucault to Church*

John D. Caputo, *What Would Jesus Deconstruct? The Good News of Postmodernism for the Church*

GloboChrist

*The Great Commission Takes
a Postmodern Turn*

Carl Raschke

Baker Academic
a division of Baker Publishing Group
Grand Rapids, Michigan

© 2008 by Carl Raschke

Published by Baker Academic
a division of Baker Publishing Group
P.O. Box 6287, Grand Rapids, MI 49516-6287
www.bakeracademic.com

Printed in the United States of America

Library of Congress Cataloging-in-Publication Data
Raschke, Carl A.
    GloboChrist : the geat commission takes a postmodern turn : the church and postmodern culture / Carl Raschke.
       p.   cm.
    Includes bibliographical references and index.
    ISBN 978-0-8010-3261-5 (pbk.)
       1. Mass media in missionary work. 2. Communication—Religious aspects—Christianity. 3. Postmodernism—Religious aspects—Christianity. 4. Globaliza-tion—Religious aspects—Christianity. I. Title.
    BV2082.M3R37 2008
    261—dc22   2008003933

To the memory of Douglas Strube,
whose inestimable friendship, missionary heart,
unflagging loyalty,
and heroic but unsuccessful struggle against cancer
inspired me to write *GloboChrist*

Contents

Series Preface   8

Series Editor's Foreword   10

Acknowledgments   14

Introduction   15

1. Globopomo: The Planetary Postmodern Moment   23

2. De-Signs of the Time   47

3. Utter Holiness or Wholly Otherness: Finding Fidelity among the Infidels   74

4. A Closer Look through the 10/40 Window   94

5. Radical Relationality: The Church in the Postmodern Cosmopolis   116

6. And Then the End Will Come   134

7. A Concluding Unacademic Postscript   151

Index   171

Series Preface

Current discussions in the church—from emerging "postmodern" congregations to mainline "missional" congregations—are increasingly grappling with philosophical and theoretical questions related to postmodernity. In fact, it could be argued that developments in postmodern theory (especially questions of "post-foundationalist" epistemologies) have contributed to the breakdown of former barriers between evangelical, mainline, and Catholic faith communities. Postliberalism—a related "effect" of postmodernism—has engendered a new, confessional ecumenism wherein we find nondenominational evangelical congregations, mainline Protestant churches, and Catholic parishes all wrestling with the challenges of postmodernism and drawing on the culture of postmodernity as an opportunity for rethinking the shape of our churches.

This context presents an exciting opportunity for contemporary philosophy and critical theory to "hit the ground," so to speak, by allowing high-level work in postmodern theory to serve the church's practice—including all the kinds of congregations and communions noted above. The goal of this series is to bring together high-profile theorists in continental philosophy and contemporary theology to write for a broad, nonspecialist audience interested in the impact of postmodern theory on the faith and practice of the church. Each book in the series will, from different angles and with different questions, undertake to answer questions such as What does postmodern theory have to say about the shape of the church? How should concrete, in-the-pew and on-the-ground religious practices be impacted by postmodernism? What should the church look like in postmodernity? What has Paris to do with Jerusalem?

The series is ecumenical not only with respect to its ecclesial destinations but also with respect to the facets of continental philosophy and theory that are represented. A wide variety of theoretical commitments will be included, ranging from deconstruction to Radical Orthodoxy, including voices from Badiou to Žižek and the usual suspects in between (Nietzsche, Heidegger, Levinas, Derrida, Foucault, Irigaray, Rorty, and others). Insofar as postmodernism occasions a retrieval of ancient sources, these contemporary sources will be brought into dialogue with Augustine, Irenaeus, Aquinas, and other resources. Drawing on the wisdom of established scholars in the field, the series will provide accessible introductions to postmodern thought with the specific aim of exploring its impact on ecclesial practice. The books are offered, one might say, as French lessons for the church.

Series Editor's Foreword

To shamelessly lift a line from a sequined and bell-bottomed Barbara Mandrell, Carl Raschke was "pomo" long before pomo was cool. Since the mid-1970s he has been on the vanguard of those engaging continental theory with an interest in not only theology but also the shape of lived religion "on the ground." In short, he was doing the work envisioned by the Church and Postmodern Culture series since before I even knew how to spell "church." So it is a distinct honor to welcome *GloboChrist* as the third volume in the series, a fitting follow-up to his groundbreaking book, *The Next Reformation*.

Judging from the book, however, Carl might want to consider becoming a fervent devotee of "remnant" theology—committed to the sense that God is present with the "few" who remain faithful—because this little manifesto is bound to shrink the circle of friends at his next dinner party. But its strident voice, which is an equal-opportunity offender on both the "left" and "right," is also its virtue. It is precisely his fierce independence of thought that makes Raschke such an important voice in current discussions about the shape of the church's mission in our "postmodern moment." As Raschke puts it, he is out to counter "those who are giddy to believe that a new kind of Christian is simply an easier-to-get-along-with Christian" (160). Contrary to those who espouse a postmodern account of mission or evangelism as a cover for engaging in "transformative dialogue" (or various other technical translations of *kumbaya*), the core argument of *GloboChrist* suggests that the church's missional task in postmodernity is inevitably a vocation of conflict. "The fulfillment of the Great Commission will not be without struggle," Raschke argues. "Through dialogue, Muslims and Christians may come to agree on common points of their mutual Abrahamic faiths, but the differences will always outweigh the similarities. The differences make the difference" (115).

Ironically, much that we get in the name of postmodern attentiveness to "difference" and "the Other" turns out to be a very timid, bland, apologetic stance that is rather embarrassed by difference and instead seeks ways, Rodney King–like, for us to all just get along. Indeed, much that traffics under this banner would be embarrassed by the very project of missions and evangelism. In short, postmodern valorization of difference has come to mean a veritable end of missions. But such responses are working out the very modern logic of toleration articulated by Locke, Kant, and others, whereas Raschke is articulating a more thoroughly postmodern account of mission that takes difference seriously enough to own up to the conflict it entails. In Raschke's project, Deleuze supersedes Derrida (21); his is an agonistic account of mission.

But most importantly, Raschke argues that a postmodern account of mission needs to flow from the logic of the incarnation. Just as God becomes enfleshed and contextualized in and for a particular time and a particular place—"born of a woman, under the law" in the "fullness of time" (Gal. 4:4), suffering "under Pontius Pilate"— so too is the church called to extend this incarnational presence. That is the nature of the *missio Dei*: not the communication of "messages" or the proliferation of programs—not even the planting of churches. It might not even be primarily about communicating some "truth" to those who are without it. Rather, it is about *being* Christ to and for the world. In a way that echoes both Kierkegaard and Bonhoeffer (fellow Lutherans in spirit with Raschke), Raschke suggests that this call to incarnational mission might require that we jettison some cherished distinctions (and fears). "Incarnational ministry in a globopomo setting," he argues, "means setting aside even the Christian/non-Christian distinction, particularly when being a Christian turns out to be a barrier to being Christ to one another" (65). Mission is above all a project of radical translation; are we

willing to let that translation escape the grammar and syntax of
our eurocentric idioms?

The "globopomo turn" for the Great Commission is occasioned by
two important realities. First, as Raschke rightly notes, postmodernism and globalization are inextricably linked. While European and
North American (especially academic) discussions of postmodern
theory tend to restrict it to the safe but largely sequestered environs
of epistemology, in fact postmodernity is synonymous with the "flattening" of the world by globalization. The postmodern moment,
as Raschke puts it, is a *global* one: "Becoming postmodern means
that we all, whether we like it or not, are now going global, which
is what that obscure first-century sect leader from Palestine truly
had in mind" (25). We can't *not* be postmodern precisely because
we can't *not* be global(ized). So postmodernism isn't about whether
we'll serve fair trade coffee at our image-driven worship events aimed
at the "creative class" in the "bobo" quarter of the city. Postmodernism isn't just a phenomenon of interest to the educated class of
Western culture or just a topic of conversation for tenured radicals
taken with continental philosophy. Rather, it is bound up with the
global conflicts and reorganizations that dominate world affairs
and foreign policy. The realities of postmodernism are grappled
with by Amnesty International and the UN, not just the Society for
Phenomenology and Existential Philosophy. And so the question
of Christian faith and postmodernism is about how Christian faith
can be communicated and lived out in a world of mass migration,
persistent genocide, increased gaps in global wealth distribution,
and the growth of global Islam.

That brings us to the second reality that needs to be faced by the
Great Commission: Islam, which is a central and persistent topic
of *GloboChrist*. Only North American Christians will find the centrality of Islam in this book to perhaps be strange or surprising;
Christians throughout the rest of the world, including Europe, know
exactly what Raschke is talking about. While it is too often reduced
to cases like headscarves in France or Turkey or the role of sharia law
in the UK, Christians in England and Germany, India and Indonesia,
are acutely aware of the role played by Islam both internationally
and domestically, precisely because Islam offers nothing short of a
comprehensive "world-and-life view" that refuses to be sequestered
as some kind of weekend hobby. Raschke's book is singular in rec-

ognizing this unique challenge, as well as in his forthright appraisals of what this means for the West and for Christianity in particular.

While there can be further conversation about his particular conclusions (whereas Raschke tends to lean on Bernard Williams and Olivier Roy, I want to at least give a hearing to Tariq Ramadan and John Esposito), I think he's exactly right to put this question at the center of discussion—to name the elephant that is in the room for Christian missions around the globe (and perhaps the elephant that will makes itself felt in the United States sooner rather than later). The result is an interesting interplay. On the one hand, Raschke unapologetically asserts a radical difference between the visions and eschatologies of Christianity and Islam in tones that I find somewhat refreshing even as (and perhaps because) I find they make me uncomfortable. On the other hand, his analysis notes that Islam is critical of Western consumerist culture in just the way the Western church *needs* to. be if it is actually going to be a witness to the coming kingdom in our postmodern world. As Raschke rightly notes, "In the West, Christians themselves cannot be a counterforce to the trend toward radical Islamism in the 10/40 Window unless they come to terms with their own spiritual weakness and the way the gospel has been compromised for the sake of the greatest of all consumerist idols—'relevance'" (108). *GloboChrist*, and the Christ that is pointed to in *GloboChrist*, calls us to nothing less than a life of radical global discipleship, to take up our cross and follow "the true Messiah and true Caesar—who reigned *because* he had conquered death by undergoing the horrifying and humiliating fate of crucifixion" (123), who now lives and reigns as a genuine emperor of a heavenly cosmopolis made immanent in us, who are called to be "Christs to each other" (65).

James K. A. Smith
York, England
Lent 2008

Acknowledgments

I would like to acknowledge the following for their support and help in this book: my wonderful wife, Sunny, first of all people who encourage me and support me to fulfill the purpose that God has fashioned me for and for which we are joined together; Aaron Sokoll, my master's student at the University of Denver, who helped me in the summer of 2006 with detailed and vital research; Joy Tienzo and Consuelo Bennett, assistants to the chair for the religious studies department, who helped me structure my time and responsibilities to finish this manuscript on time; Bob Hosack of Baker Academic, who has pushed forward both this work and my previous one with Baker Academic; and my other students at the University of Denver who have been engaged in this new and exciting conversation about what globalization really means.

Introduction

We must be global Christians with a global vision
because our God is a global God.

John Stott

If future historians ever decide on what book from present or
recent times most compactly epitomized the rise and fall of the
postmodern world, it will be probably be Francis Fukuyama's *The
End of History and the Last Man*.[1] Published in 1992, Fukuyama's
well-known work prophesied that the collapse of Communism
certified the world historical triumph of liberal democracy and
global capitalism. Fukuyama borrowed the phrase "end of history" from the nineteenth-century German philosopher G. W. F.
Hegel. Hegel had regarded history as a struggle, or dialectic, between opposing ideas. The struggle between systems of ideas—or
ideologies—had defined both the twentieth century's war against
fascism and the Cold War.

Now that this ideological tousle was over, the world could gin-
gerly but confidently stride into this new neoliberal millennium.
The next century, he insinuated, would be a time when individuals the world over would be at last free to cultivate, express, and

---

1. Francis Fukuyama, *The End of History and the Last Man* (repr.; New York:
Free Press, 2006).

develop themselves as individuals and to achieve the kind of recognition that authoritarian and totalitarian political structures since the beginnings of history had denied them. It was their natural right to do so. Not only was deadly conflict at an end but also history itself, Fukuyama assured us, insofar as by "history" we mean the repeated dashing of deep desires, dreams, and hopes on the part of the human species by the machinelike apparatus of state violence and counterviolence. In many ways Fukuyama's prophecy, which turned out to be false, also constituted a false dawn. Looking back we can say that it betokened a false promise that the End—not just the terminus but the goal—of history would be as peaceful and easy as the bloodless events of 1989–91, and that the fulfillment of myriad natural longings and ambitions—the presumed purpose of liberal democracy—consisted in the end of human existence itself.

For many at the time, the early 1990s amounted to what in this book I will call the "postmodern moment." It was the moment when all the past convictions and ideological certitudes had been deconstructed by what Hegelians themselves came to term the "cunning of history." In the decade that followed this, neoliberalism, riding on the postmodern wave of the new history that Fukuyama had called the end of history, seemed unstoppable. The wave itself, which came to be known as globalization, brought in its wake unforeseen and unintended consequences. One of these consequences was the fostering of a new world disorder resulting from massive migrations of people, the proliferation of local wars and failed states, and stark contrasts between rapid economic growth in some regions and among certain populations, and appalling poverty and misery among others. It was not a neoliberal utopia, as Fukuyama had predicted, but a kind of dystopia, with a different set of descriptors and predictors.

In the early 1990s two major intellectual figures had the first inklings of a different vision of the new globalizing world. They were the French philosopher Jacques Derrida, the architect of postmodernist thought, and the American political scientist Samuel Huntington. Derrida talked about the "return of religion." Huntington envisaged what he termed "the clash of civilizations." Huntington's description was drawn from a clash of global value systems anchored in conflicting religious belief structures. After 9/11 the world woke up to realize that it had achieved the new, and perhaps true, postmodern moment. What was at stake was no longer economic prosperity but ultimate truth anchored in the claims of faith.

I have written this book for the world, but its immediate audience is America, especially religious America and the church in America, and particularly the American evangelical Christian church. It is about globalization and how it is bringing about an end of history that no one in the early 1990s could imagine. It is not so much about the clash of civilizations as it is about a "clash of revelations"—an expression that will become less opaque as the book progresses— and what that means for this unique postmodern moment that we are experiencing.

Unfortunately, many in the West chronically fail to connect the dots when it comes to comprehending the drastic social and political upheavals as well as the dramatic global changes that hit the headline news everyday—and that is even more painfully true for Christians in the West. The West's "dominant culture"—a term often used by those on the left to denigrate the historic constellation of middle-class values and libertarian politics—supplies effective blinders. But the left in the West, increasingly led by antiglobal-ization and antimilitary activists as well as the green movement, is often unaware that it is wearing the same blinders. Whether it tilts to the left or to the right, the dominant culture of the West since the eighteenth century has been secular and individualistic, convinced that the supreme goal of human life and human history is the private pursuit of happiness and the guarantee of distinct individual political rights.

Fukuyama's failed prophecy was founded on the giddy assump-tion, during the immediate post-Communist era, that the spread of democratic capitalism along with bourgeoning incomes and height-ened consumer options for the world's impoverished masses would assuage the violence and social conflicts generated in the past by the militant ideologies of modern times. But those who denounced this version of neoliberalism by pointing out its fraudulent utopianism while decrying the social injustices wrought by the relentless march of market economies and international corporate interests were shouting into the wind as well. Even today in the West, progres-sives and conservatives alike miss the broader and deeper trajectory of events. They scarcely recognize that what Huntington termed "the rest" of the world is in an open and increasingly antagonistic struggle with the West. They also miss the point that the struggle is not anti-Western per se. It is primarily antisecular and therefore only anti-Western in the sense that the West has made secularity its dominant culture, displacing, and in many cases renouncing, its Judeo-Christian heritage.

What does the foregoing have to do with postmodernism? The adjective *postmodern*, in its uncounted usages and syntactical peculiarities, has reflected a mood brewing for almost two generations that a once-triumphal secular West, with its mission to modernize the rest of the planet, has been unraveling, if not in its ability to project its money and its might, then at least in its self-confidence about what it ultimately stands for. *Postmodern* is not a word that merely applies to a certain well-publicized, widely celebrated, and generically French company of faddish philosophers and religious thinkers. As a luxuriant popular and academic literature on our postmodern condition makes clear, the expression signifies something epochal and world-defining, something that reminds us, in a paraphrase of Shakespeare, that there is "more in heaven and earth than is imagined in [our] philosophy."[2] Our postmodern era also signals the arrival of a *post-Western* era. But "post-Western" does not necessarily mean that the heritage of the West has sunk into the shadows. Much of the globe has now absorbed that heritage. Just as the eclipse of ancient Rome was followed by the rise of a new Roman civilization that was predominantly Germanic but subsequently came to be called European, so the decline of the West will likely lead to a new world that remains Western in character, though no longer in name. Furthermore, in the same way that the new and powerful faith that came to be known as Christianity both survived and transformed the old Roman Empire, so the same faith, contrary to what anyone would have expected less than a generation ago, is both outlasting the West and undergoing a dramatic *global* metamorphosis. This change is due not so much to the abiding influence of the West as to the mysterious power of Christ—what we really mean by *GloboChrist*—that has been subtly shaping and directing human history toward its consummation throughout the ages and, theologically speaking, is traceable back to the promise given to Abraham.

Westerners, especially evangelical Protestants, may be uncomfortable with this way of speaking. After all, doesn't it all come down

2. Shakespeare, *Hamlet*, act 1, scene 5, lines 174–75.

to the person of Jesus and our relationship to him? Yet in the final analysis it depends on what we mean by the "person." The Christian God is a *personal* God. His power lies in his personhood, in his capacity for relationship, not just in his action. In that respect one can say, at the risk of misunderstanding, that for Christians the power of our God lies in his *power of relationship*, or the power of establishing, sustaining, and purposefully pursuing relationships. His is a power in this sense, not just an impersonal force. The *GloboChrist* is a theological term we have coined to show how this power is manifesting itself amid the growing anxieties over what is happening under the impact of the force we call globalization and the political, cultural, and religious upheavals that arise in its wake. Christ is showing his power not just among the nations but also for the nations. Christ, as Martin Luther expressed it, is never God "in himself." He is always God "for us" (*für uns*) and "with us" (*mit uns*). He is *Emmanuel*, meaning the God of relation. This power of relationship is affirmed in the Nicene Creed, the confessional benchmark for all believers. He is one nature (Greek: *ousia*; Latin: *substantia*), three "persons" (Greek: *hypostases*; Latin: *personae*). Far more than Roman Catholicism and Western Protestantism (which has its own Latin origins), Eastern Orthodoxy has stressed the relational character of God, or at least the relationality that is existential and incarnational rather than strictly intellectual and conceptual.

We can discern this difference when we contrast Augustine of Hippo's formulation of the doctrine of the Trinity with that of Eastern Orthodoxy. In *De Trinitate*, composed in the early fifth century, Augustine undertakes a theological exposition of what his contemporaries considered the mystery of the Trinity by resorting to an analogy from philosophical psychology taken from Neoplatonism. God is best understood as the Great *Nous*, or eternal mind. The components of mind are relational. Thus, Augustine writes, "we find in memory, understanding, and will a triad of certainties with regard to the nature of the mind. They present a single, substantial reality, in differing relations to itself."[3] But in orthodoxy, deriving from the Cappadocian fathers of the fourth century, the emphasis is more on the *energeia*, or operations, of God, necessitating a doctrine of *concrete and dynamic relationality*. All trinitarian talk, as one orthodox

3. Augustine, *Later Works*, trans. John Burnaby (Philadelphia: Westminster, 1960), 72.

author puts it, "implies a movement of mutual love."[4] As globalization accelerates, therefore, and Christianity becomes less and less a
Western religion (which it never was in the beginning), can we not
begin to see this dynamic and incarnational relationality of the Trinity
in time and history itself? Is not this time in which we are now living
full, or pregnant (the implication of the biblical term *kairos*), with
God's profound and hidden purpose? Are there not millions of new
Christians around the world—unlike us jaded, oversophisticated, and
secularized Westerners—who take this time as indicating the triumph
of the church universal to be the manifestation of Christ's global
body? Like Paul, they "consider that the sufferings of this present
time are not worth comparing with the glory about to be revealed to
us. For the creation waits in eager expectation for the revealing of the
children of God" (Rom. 8:18–19 NRSV). Is that not what is implied in
the teaching that the Word became flesh? Is that not just the historical
but also the eschatological meaning of "incarnation"?

Relational Christianity *is* postmodern Christianity. Unfortunately,
among both proponents and critics alike, the idea of the postmodern
has become too easily and almost exclusively identified with the
sort of philosophical and theological iconoclasm that has come to
be popularly known as "deconstruction," even though when the
term was formulated in French philosophy back in the early 1970s it
had a very narrow and technical set of indexes. In Christian circles
much of this iconoclasm has been directed against the evangelical
establishment and the politics of the religious right, the usual target of scorn among academics. But those ongoing rhetorical barks
are starting to lose their bite and perhaps even beginning to bore.
The postmodern moment is far more momentous than the cultural
spleen and political partisanship that has defined much of Western
discourse for nearly half a century.

The first chapter of this book analyzes why this postmodern
moment in history is a global one, what I term "globopomo." It
profiles and analyzes the social and historical phenomenon that
has been gaining so much attention quite recently—the rise of the
"global South" and the way it is totally transfiguring the geography
of Christianity as well as its methods of theological thinking and
religious practice, particularly the practice of missions.

4. Bishop Kallistos (Timothy Ware) of Diokleia, *The Orthodox Way* (Crestwood,
NY: St. Vladimir's Seminary Press, 1995), 33.

Chapter 2 investigates the new postmodern way of envisioning missions. It ties the new incarnational theology to the work of missions, essentially arguing that missions must become, and is becoming, "missional" in the sense that the word has come to be deployed. It gives some illustrations of how emerging Christians, who have taken up the cause of being both missional and relevant, can start to imagine how they can become both more missional and more relevant in a global context. Finally, it offers a different take on what postmodernist philosophical resources might come into play for taking this incarnational turn. It calls our attention to the work of Gilles Deleuze and the semiotic project as superseding Derrida and the all-too-familiar deconstructionist project.

Chapter 3 discusses how the incarnational turn reflects historic Christianity's tendency to be semiotically supple and to indigenize the gospel. It argues that Christianity has always been incarnational in this ongoing way. From the first century onward, Christianity was incarnating in the cultural forms and sign systems that it encountered. The incorporation of the language of the Mediterranean mystery religions into the early Christian vocabulary is a case in point. It is similar to what is happening today in the global South. Christianity has become indigenized and hence globalized through its multifaceted, native, and "pagan" expressions. It has clothed itself—and turned that clothing inside out as it did in ancient and medieval times—in everything from spirit healing to demon exorcism and ancestor worship.

Chapter 4, however, delineates where Christianity's capacity to indigenize runs up against a concrete barrier. This barrier is the Islamic world, which is undergoing a revival of a magnitude not seen since the sixteenth century. Until quite recently Christian missionaries have innocuously referred to this region of the world as the 10/40 Window, indicating the general latitudes between which it is so difficult to evangelize. Yet since 9/11 there has been a slowly growing recognition that the challenge is not simply evangelism, which Islam historically and forcefully resists. The genuine question is how the new globalized Christianity will contend with the new globalized Islam, which is a product of virtually the same historical forces. This book argues that both Christianity and Islam are competing globalizing forces driven by a universalistic faith that commences with the story of Abraham but diverges in its meaning and import. The chapter concludes with an exhortation to Christians to take their faith as seriously as the jihadists do, becoming the "church militant" in the original sense of the phrase, without the military, and in a postmodern way.

Chapter 5 asks what a reinvented, postmodern, global evangelical Christianity would turn out to be. It outlines four R's of a Christianity that is faithful to the Great Commission in today's globopomo cosmopolis. It calls for a Christianity that is radical, relational, revelatory, and "rhizomic"—a word that Gilles Deleuze deployed to characterize the new global, postmodern organizations that the church must emulate. It contrasts the radical relationality of Christianity with the transcendental moral collectivism offered by current globo-socialist visionaries along with Islamism (the new and aggressive form of political Islam) all of which are vying for adherents.

Chapter 6 deals with a subject that is usually scanted by contemporary theological writers—eschatology or the anticipation of the "end times"—even though pop eschatology for some time has been all the rage. In its eschatology the global commitment of a faith is sealed. The chapter contrasts the eschatologies of Christianity and Islam. Eschatology not only frames the motivations of various peoples of faith but also charts the field for the expansion of faith in a global setting. A new eschatology is emerging that envisions the radical relationality of the Christ who is returning, the GloboChrist, one that will reactivate the summons of the Great Commission in this day and age.

Chapter 7 takes a look at both current advocates and critics of what is normally termed "postmodern Christianity." It finds both versions wanting in key respects, mainly because of their Western parochialism, which can be both overt and subtle. It concludes that to understand the dynamics of future faith, we must truly think globally even if we act locally.

1

Globopomo

The Planetary Postmodern Moment

> The speed of light does not merely transform the world. It becomes the world. Globalization is the speed of light.
>
> Paul Virilio

Christianity's Postmodern Moment

After centuries of strife between orthodoxies and heresies, religious wars over sectarian issues, and the multiplication of denominations founded on different interpretations of Holy Writ, sacrament, morality, and tradition, the West is no longer the Christian West in any recognizable guise. Christianity has passed from the West to the "rest" of the world. Christianity is no longer merely a Western phenomenon but is instead a global one. As Christians we are now all part of a new body of Christ, the *GloboChrist*. GloboChristianity is the decisive trend of the late postmodern era that is sweeping us beyond the postmodern. While the increasing tension in the American churches between moderns and postmoderns has deteriorated into the latest and greatest variant on the tireless and tiresome battle of social styles and political values that have come to be known as the culture wars, global Christians are laying down their lives—as Jesus called them to do—for fellow believers in the most extreme situations. The issue is not whether one should go to church anymore, or whether church is "relevant"; it is about whether one can go to church without being imprisoned, beaten, or tortured.

Christianity as a motivating cultural force in Western civilization, mainly in Europe but also to a surprising degree in the United States, is largely spent. Yet all across the developing—the so-called postcolonial—world, Christianity is rapidly gaining both traction and surprising momentum. This slow Christianizing of countries previously non-Christian—or decidedly anti-Christian, in the case of the former Communist bloc—at the same time that secular market economies are also taking hold cannot be explained simply as the result of Occidental precedents and influences. Indian Christianity, for example, looks a lot more like archaic Hindu devotional movements than like Roman Catholicism or mainline Protestantism. Latin American Pentecostalism, which is undermining the centuries-old alliance of regional politics with the Catholic clergy, resembles more the messianic religious nativism that challenged Spanish colonial administrations in the seventeenth century than it does the nineteenth-century cartel of the church and the ruling European oligarchies.[1] Chinese Christianity may soon reach ten percent of the population—approximately the same portion of Christians in the Roman Empire when Constantine converted in the early fourth century and made the faith of Jesus's followers into the official state religion—and has almost as many complex and diverse characteristics as the culture and politics of Asia's great dragon (China).[2] In Africa, Christianity

    1. See, e.g., R. Andrew Chestnut, *Born Again in Brazil: The Pentecostal Boom and the Pathogens of Poverty* (New Brunswick, NJ: Rutgers University Press, 1997); David Stoll, *Is Latin America Turning Protestant? The Politics of Evangelical Growth* (Berkeley: University of California Press, 1990); André Corten and Ruth Marshall-Fratani, eds., *Between Babel and Pentecost: Transnational Pentecostalism in Africa and Latin America* (Bloomington: Indiana University Press, 2001); Joel Robbins, "The Globalization of Pentecostal and Charismatic Christianity," *Annual Review of Anthropology* 33 (2004): 117–43; Virginia Garrard-Burnett, "The Third Church in Latin America: Religion and Globalization in Contemporary Latin America," *Latin American Research Review* 39 (October 2004): 257–69.

    2. See David Aikman, *Jesus in Beijing: How Christianity Is Transforming China and Changing the Global Balance of Power* (New York: Regnery, 2006); Stephen Uhalley and Xiaoxin Wu, eds., *China and Christianity: Burdened Past, Hopeful Future* (Armonk, NY: M. E. Sharpe, 2001). For historical overviews, see George H. Dunne, SJ, *A Generation*

has been the most influential force—perhaps surpassing even Western capitalism itself—in promoting modernization and the development of institutions and communications systems that we assume are simply the outgrowth of globalization.[3]

Christianity in general and Christian missions specifically have come to a pivot in world history that seems as unprecedented as the transformation of Caesar's realm during the first three centuries of the common era. That change came through the strange and distinctly un-Roman cult from Palestine centering on the crucifixion and resurrection of a mysterious nobody now known to history as Jesus of Nazareth. Let us call it the church's postmodern moment. Contrary to carping old-guard evangelicals, becoming postmodern is not some Bohemian lifestyle choice, or heretical outrage, among twenty- and thirty-something young theologians, even though many who claim that mantle unfortunately are living up to the caricature foisted on them. Becoming postmodern means that we all, whether we like it or not, are now going global, which is what that obscure first-century sect leader from Palestine truly had in mind.

The postmodern moment in Christianity arrives at a time when Jesus's command to his followers to "make disciples of all nations"— the so-called Great Commission—is having a profound impact beyond the geographical zone in which Christianity was spawned and grew to maturity. Postmodernity not only coincides with the advent of a genuine global Christianity, it also is the propulsive force. How do we account for this incredible turn of events?

There are a number of obvious and not-so-obvious factors that are responsible for the emergence of a postmodern GloboChristianity, the formation of an authentically catholic faith in Christ, for whom there is "no east or west" as well as "no south or north," as runs the hymn. The new GloboChrist is neither the Jesus historically pictured through Western eyes nor the variety of formerly indigenous Christs

of Giants (London: Burns & Oates, 1962); Suzanne W. Barnett and John King Fairbank, China in Christianity: Early Protestant Missionary Writings (Cambridge, MA: Harvard University Press and The Council on East Asian Studies, 1985).

3. See Richard Gray, Black Christians and White Missionaries (New Haven: Yale University Press, 1990). For further insight about the new African Christianity, see Allan Anderson, "New African Initiated Pentecostalism and Charismatics in South Africa," Journal of Religion in Africa 35 (2005): 66–92; Birgit Meyer, "Christianity in Africa: From African Independent to Pentecostal-Charismatic Churches," Annual Review of Anthropology 33 (2004): 447–74.

from sundry native traditions who perhaps often had more pagan than biblical traits. Nor is our GloboChrist the ecumenical fusion of various evangelical, orthodox, liberal, liberation, or race-based theo-ideologies that have been elaborated from the fertile, constructive minds of seminary-trained Christian professionals and academics. The coming of the GloboChrist is far better appreciated by anthropologists and historians of religion, who happen to be specialists in cultural sign-systems and the various subtleties of the symbol-making processes, than it is by church theologians. One must de-theologize the complex legacy from different denominations about missions and evangelism, even to a certain extent the now-fashionable talk about "missional" Christianity in a postmodern context.

Much of the missional and "emerging" talk about evangelical post-Christendom is much more parochial, Eurocentric, and less radical than even so-called progressive evangelicals tend to think.[4] The idea of post-Christendom often turns out to be simply a current version of what H. Richard Niebuhr termed the "Christ of culture," in this instance postmodern urban culture.[5] The truly radical shift presently under way is the deconstruction of all cultural Christs through the interpenetration of a welter of highly modernized social configurations with differing religious practices by the power of a gospel message that has little theological baggage on this new global turf in comparison with all the conceptual and symbolic freight the same discourse has acquired in the West. One can guess that the same power was at work in the first-century Levant. Although Christianity initially arose as a sectarian movement that appealed primarily to Jews in their Diaspora in the Roman Empire, it was able to overleap—even apart from Paul's missionary genius—vast cultural chasms in a brief time span.

4. For a good overview of what missional Christianity means, see Darrell L. Guder, *Missional Church: A Vision for the Sending of the Church in North America* (Grand Rapids: Eerdmans, 1998).

5. Take, for example, Stuart Murray's well-known book *Post-Christendom* (Carlisle, UK: Paternoster, 2004). Murray talks extensively about the decline of the church in the West and advocates a kind of return to the Radical Reformation legacy of the sixteenth century, particularly the Anabaptist movement, from which his own heritage springs. He "reimagines" a post-Christendom church that includes "poets and mystical dreamers" as opposed to technically trained clergy. He also sees Christianity as a kind of "re-marginalization" of the faith, as it is already in the West. But Murray says virtually nothing about the dynamism of a new global Christianity that is going in certain areas in a reverse direction, from margins to mainstream.

Postmodernism as a historical and cultural phenomenon—as opposed to a philosophical, theological, or intellectual worldview as it is usually construed by American scholars—has been defined by the contemporary Russian political scientist D. A. Silichev as the era when "modernist Eurocentrism" is rapidly being "replaced with . . . global polycentrism."[6] Today, "globalization" is a much-used and rather slippery term, but it is clear that whatever it represents, we are in the midst of it. According to Silichev, globalization "is a world community minus a world state and world governance; it is a Net in which ideas about the guiding and the guided have no real meaning."[7] A more useful definition has been provided by Ellen Frost. She characterizes it as a "long-term process of connection and transformation" that "sets in motion a living, expanding, and highly uneven network of cross-border flows" from goods and services to people and ideas.[8] What do globalization and postmodernism have to do with each other? Everything. They are not cultural or moral choices that peoples and individuals in different societies everywhere on the planet casually make.

At the same time, the same peoples and individuals do not have the easy option of deciding *not* to be postmodern any more than they can simply elect to send a message between New York and Botswana by telegraph or to travel from San Francisco to Singapore by steamship the way it was done a century ago. As we know with the case of the Amish, entire ethnic or religious groups can refuse to deploy certain up-to-date technologies out of concern that their beliefs and values will also be severely compromised.

But no one can refuse to be postmodern any more than one can resolve to live completely as people did in the seventeenth century, unless we are talking about hermits or geographically isolated tribes in the jungles of Southeast Asia or New Guinea. One of the critical connotations of postmodernity, according to Silichev's definition, is that globalization coincides with localization. And previously localized, or parochial, habits now have a worldwide fascination and currency. Increasingly uniform economic and communication

6. Quoted by Igor Petrov in "Globalization as a Postmodern Phenomenon," *International Affairs: A Russian Journal of World Politics, Diplomacy and International Relations* 49 (2003): 127.

7. Ibid., 129.

8. Ellen Frost, "From Rockets to Religion: Understanding Globalization," working paper, European Union Studies Center, October 6, 2000.

systems are matched—ironically—by distinct and particular cultural expressions, even if none of them can be considered "native" or "traditional" any longer. An obvious example is the vast array of ethnic foods that have become available to global consumers from Kansas City to Berlin because of the transnational flows of capital investment and high-tech marketing.

Postmodernization and Globalization

According to the twentieth-century French postmodernist philosopher Gilles Deleuze, who recognized this sort of trend long before social theorists did at the opening of the new millennium, globalization is a feature not only of cultures and economies but also of the very tools of communication we use to understand one another. Verbal, visual, behavioral, and structural complexes of signs—studied by various specialists under the rubric of the science of semiotics (from the Greek *sēmeion* for "sign")—become "globo-local," insofar as they impart certain mixed messages that secure for different peoples a sense of personal identity and uniqueness, when all identities throughout the world are up for grabs. The visible processes of globalization make us aware of the erasure of all fixed linguistic and social boundaries that is now occurring.

In the 1980s a global polling organization tried to discover what was the most recognized face on the planet. The result was startling. It was not the face of President Reagan, the pope, or even Chairman Mao of China, who had just recently died. It was not an iconic picture of Jesus or the Buddha. It was that of Colonel Sanders, founder of Kentucky Fried Chicken restaurants that were now ubiquitous throughout the developed and developing worlds. Kentucky Fried Chicken, a product with a narrowly regional name when it was introduced into the market with all the cachet that might imply, is now simply KFC, which doesn't even communicate the fact that the product it sells is poultry.

The face of the colonel and the familiar brand abbreviation have no reality in themselves. They are "pure signs," what the postmodern French philosopher and media theorist Jean Baudrillard terms "simulacra." Deleuze calls this total transformation of linguistic meaning the play of two complementary processes: "deterritorialization" and "reterritorialization." Globalization is at once the abolition of territorial limits and the creation of new symbolic boundaries that are easily and swiftly erased in the twinkling of an eye—or the launching of a new planetary media campaign. Globalization is no longer about what and where so much as it is about whatever and wherever.

The map is no longer even the territory, because neither map nor territory can any longer be defined or delimited. For example, in the latter part of the first decade of the new millennium, Europe looks more like the Middle Ages than it did only a few years ago. The change has little to do with the recent implementation of a "united states" of Europe, known today as the European Union. Just as in the eleventh century, before sovereign states existed, territories were generally marked by where the presence or military influence of a certain prince might be obvious, so a thousand years later the entire patchwork is rapidly becoming deterritorialized by mobile labor and intricate patterns of cultural exchange. We really know where Germany "is" only because a certain language is spoken there and certain various tourist attractions are there. No longer is there a British Empire on which "the sun never sets." But the new empire of English as the lingua franca for all commercial transactions is vastly more extensive than when Queen Victoria raised her scepter and nations cowered.

But what is true of consumer products and services is also true of their spiritual counterparts. The globalization of religion is inseparable from the globalization of the marketplace. And as in the marketplace, certain consumer products tend to catch on more than others. During the height of the Cold War, in the West and in the second world of Russian military power and diplomacy, both godless American capitalism and godless Communism—celebrated during the death-of-God movement in the mainstream Protestant seminaries in the 1960s—assumed that they had rendered religion obsolete. At that time the newly perceived beginnings of globalization were interpreted as Westernization, equaling modernization, which equaled secularization. A God-diminished modernizing world seemed ready to run roughshod over all forms of strong religious faith, which were supposedly confined to enclaves of cultural backwardness in the Indian subcontinent or the American Bible Belt.

But a funny thing happened during the march of a now-economically interdependent humanity toward a brave new world of triumphal secularity. The fall of the Soviet Union in 1989 was not so much an enduring victory for democratic capitalism over Marxism as it was the first loud report in the clamorous collapse of the vision of a secularized world and a religionless global politics to which Western pundits and policy makers had considered themselves to be the sole legitimate heirs.

This epochal event was followed by approximately a decade of heightened planetary prosperity fostering what turned out to be a false consensus that globalization meant seamless integration of peoples and ideologies powered by digital computer networks, surging market economies, the withdrawal of immigration barriers, easier and more convenient forms of travel, and bourgeoning systems of speed-of-light telecommunications. This new secularist mythology found numerous adherents, the most celebrated of which was *New York Times* columnist Thomas Friedman. In the first edition of his runaway bestseller *The World Is Flat*, Friedman proclaimed that the world five centuries after Columbus was best again perceived as it was in the fourteenth century. By the provocative metaphor of a "flat earth," Friedman suggested that the West's former political, economic, and military dominance had been suddenly and seriously challenged by the low-cost workforce and entrepreneurial dynamism of the developing world. Friedman cited the obvious examples of China and India. But he saw the "flattening" of the global economic horizon to be an unavoidable development, with uncharted consequences for the future.

Looking back, we cannot by any means conclude that Friedman got it all wrong. But what he left out, at least in the first edition published in 2005, was the way in which the religious factor, particularly radical Islamism, was starting to undermine the expectation of a global secularist utopia. In his most recent rendering of the world-is-flat thesis, Friedman makes the point that religious terrorism, particularly radical Islamism, is as much an output of globalization as the confluence of political and economic practices. Friedman writes: "Though we didn't notice it at the time, there was a discordant note in this exciting new era. It wasn't only Americans and Europeans who joined the people of the Soviet Empire in celebrating the fall of the wall. . . . Someone else was raising a glass. . . . His name was Osama bin Laden, and he had a different narrative."[9]

But Friedman still tends to see radical religiosity more as a fly buzzing on the screen door than as a deeper disturbance. The struggle

9. Thomas Friedman, *The World Is Flat: A Brief History of the Twenty-First Century* (New York: Farrar, Straus & Giroux, 2005), 58.

between emerging strains of fierce religious neoconservatism, including everything from Serbian nationalist orthodoxy to al-Qaida's campaign against the West to militant Hindu nationalism, is not necessarily a mere blip if we carefully consider what is happening everywhere today. The idea that religion is not resisting globalization as much as it is lending a whole new verve to national and ethnic particularities has been offered by Vinoth Ramachandra. According to Ramachandra, the "globalizing processes both corrode inherited cultural and personal identities and, at the same time, stimulate the revitalization of particular identities as a way of gaining more power or influence in this new global order."[10] Ramachandra points out that Christianity is itself a different sort of globalizing leaven that affects the whole loaf. He has in mind the way in which a new third-world "identity politics" uses indigenous faith to counter the secularizing inroads from the West. Christianity, he argues, appeals to those who feel disinherited by both secularization and the new religious nationalism—or in the case of Islam, transnationalism. It supplies a powerful dose of human dignity, intentional community, and personal empowerment where otherwise a lethal combination of economic exploitation and cultural caste discrimination would prevail. "The church is the only truly global community," Ramachandra writes, "and it is largely a church *of* the poor."[11]

But the postmodern configuration of religion at a global level— Christian faith or otherwise—is not as straightforward as it may appear at first glance. Postmodernism, as the very term implies, is what comes *after* modernism. Modernism has come to be associated with the European Enlightenment of the eighteenth century and the scientific assault on traditional religious conviction that gathered speed in the late nineteenth century and reached its climax in the mid-twentieth century. To its detractors—both religious and secular—postmodernism is routinely vilified as a cult of unreason and as having a tendency to take excessive liberties with language. It is also branded—quite wrongly—as a degenerate form of moral, cultural, or philosophical relativism. The sundry stereotypes in Western society of the postmodernist betray deep-reaching secular prejudices, even among many self-professed Christian believers. Postmodern-

10. Vinoth Ramachandra, "Global Religious Transformation, Political Vision, and Christian Witness," *International Review of Missions* 94 (October 2005): 482.
11. Ibid., 487.

ism is frequently satirized or condemned in such circles as a type of juvenile outrageousness, a cultural theater of the absurd.

But the global shifts that bear the stamp of the postmodern have a quite different look and feel to them. In many ways these shifts can be construed as taking issue with the assumption that to globalize is ipso facto to secularize. This same caution applies to the Islamist phenomenon as well. Islamism is generally dismissed as an effort to bring back the Middle Ages, but careful analysis of the phenomenon itself indicates the opposite. Islamism, or more technically re-Islamization, in the view of French social theorist Olivier Roy, is a distinctive third-world reaction to the European version of secularism as it plays itself out on the international stage. The Islamists "want to bridge the gap between religion and a secularized society by exacerbating the religious dimensions, overstretching it to the extent that it cannot become a habitus by being embedded in a real culture."[12] Islamism is both desecularization and a new type of secularization at the same time, because it decouples the Muslim religion from its historic and cultural base while creating a style of globalism rivaling that promoted by the West, one that at least champions the sense of non-Western identity in the same way that, paradoxically, Christianity often now does in the postcolonial era.

Contrary to the famous argument of Harvard political scientist Samuel Huntington—right after the Soviet Union unraveled, he predicted a "clash of civilizations" where the legacies of the West and the Middle East would find themselves on an unstoppable collision course—the conflict is turning out to be one between those who assert the antireligious values of modernism and the Enlightenment on one hand and those who find ways of repackaging old religious symbols for contemporary political purposes on the other. The genuine clash of civilizations is "between the religious and the non-religious," not between the different religious cultures.[13]

12. Olivier Roy, *Globalized Islam: The Search for a New Ummah* (New York: Columbia University Press, 2004), 40. For related research see Johan Meuleman, ed., *Islam in the Era of Globalization* (London: RoutledgeCurzon, 2002); Ali Mohammadi, ed., *Islam Encountering Globalization* (London: RoutledgeCurzon, 2002); Stephen Vertigans and Philip W. Sutton, "Globalisation Theory and Islamic Praxis," *Global Society* 16 (2002): 31–46.

13. Gregory Melleuish, "Globalised Religions for a Globalised World," *Policy* 21 (Winter 2005): 20. See also Robert Weller, "Afterword: On Global Nation-States and Rooted Universalisms," *European Journal of East Asian Studies* 2 (2003): 322–27.

The Resurgence of Religion

It was the now-deceased Jacques Derrida—the grand old man of postmodernism—who discerned back in the early 1990s, right after the "Huntington thesis" began to grab headlines, that something unprecedented was afoot. Long before anyone in the West had even heard of Osama bin Laden and seven years before hijacked planes destroyed New York's World Trade Center, Derrida took his postmodernist intellectual revolution one step further by proclaiming that it was not about "deconstruction," whatever kind of freight the public thought that word still carried, but about the "return of the religious."

The return of the religious, according to Derrida, is inextricably bound up with what is conventionally termed "globalization," and what Derrida himself calls "globalatinization." The latter expression sounds a bit odd to those of us who prefer to regard globalization specifically as "Westernization" in the broader connotation of the word. But Derrida makes a tacit historical comparison that has tremendous implications for any forecast about what is coming for the new global Christianity. Westernization, as we know, is driven by what Derrida, following French academic convention, describes as "tele-technoscience," the synergy between practical science and the development of far-reaching and advanced communications technology. Tele-technoscience, as the twentieth-century historian Arnold Toynbee stressed, is the present principle of world unification in the same way that the might of Roman legions two millennia ago brought about the consolidation of the civic and economic disparities of the European and Mediterranean realms. We are now in a second wave of latinization, which, as ancient history makes clear, did not really succeed until Christianity began to grow its own spiritual shadow-state within a state. The Constantinian age was not so much a dramatic break from the pagan past as it was a belated recognition on the part of the Caesars of where the new polity for a disintegrating Roman Empire was vested.

The postmodern era, Derrida suggests, represents such a second wave because it all comes down to the economic and social forces put into play at the end of the Cold War that on a global scale have led to the integration of the cultural and economic—though not necessarily the political—order of things. Derrida regards the postmodern world order as a veiled Latin imperium, a Fourth Rome in the language of classical empire-speak.[14] The primary purpose of any "Roman" empire, according to Derrida, is "pacification." In the few centuries before and in the period immediately after the birth of Jesus, Rome's influence spread as a consequence of the pervasive civil and internecine conflicts marking the breakdown of the old *koinōnia* established by Alexander the Great. The new postmodern world empire has been forged, perhaps fortuitously, by the ubiquitous clash of economic regimes everywhere on the planet, wrought by the collision of capitalism with Marxist socialism.

Nevertheless, it was not capitalism per se but tele-technoscience under the guise of global communications and the consumer-driven market economy that was the decisive factor in "winning" the Cold War, as far as such an analysis might go. We might coin a different term to describe this process: "globo-electro-Westernization." The end of Communism paved the way for genuine empire. Ironically, it is this pacification of nations in the new empire that has triggered the return of religion.

> The field of this war or of this pacification is henceforth without limit: all the religions, their centres of authority, the religious cultures, states, nations or ethnic groups that they represent have unequal access, to be sure, but often one that is immediate and potentially without limit, to the same world market. They are at the same time producers, actors and sought-after consumers, at times exploiters, at times victims. [At stake in the struggle] is thus access to world (transnational or transstate) networks of telecommunication and of tele-technoscience. Henceforth religion "in the singular" accompanies and even precedes the critical and technoscientific reason, it watches over it as its shadow.[15]

14. In classical historical parlance, the empire of the first four centuries was the First Rome, Byzantium the Second, and imperial Russia (which in the Slavic domains appropriated most of the heritage of Byzantine orthodoxy, particularly after the fall of Constantinople to the Turks in 1453) the Third. Of course, the French and German emperors of medieval Europe, beginning with Charlemagne, fashioned themselves "Holy Roman" emperors, and there is some evidence that the Abbasid caliphs of Islam, based in Baghdad, modeled themselves after the Caesars, although the comparison was far more un-Islamic than Constantine's assumption of power as a "Christian" emperor was un-Christian by the standards of their day. Finally, there is also, at least in the late 1970s and early 1980s, some suggestion that the Soviet politburo began consciously to adopt the older language of the czars as the Third Rome and to view Russian Communism in that light.

15. Jacques Derrida, *Acts of Religion*, ed. Gil Anidjar (New York: Routledge, 2002), 79.

As Derrida points out, the word *religion* comes from the Latin *religio*, meaning to "bind" or "obligate." The empire was founded on a multitude of religious practices and religious observances as a way to bind local ethnic communities into a much larger civic encomium of what scholars refer to as *Romanitas*, which was similar to today's somewhat airy ideal of global citizenship. During the first century the inauguration of Caesar worship, which the early Christians resisted with a ferocity that their pagan masters could not fathom, was an extension of this fundamental religious convention of merging spiritual observance with a demand for political loyalty. The Roman insistence on religious tolerance, which early Christianity then and radical Islamism nowadays have both rejected, was part of this equation.

Hence, postmodern religiosity is intricately enmeshed with the world market, according to Derrida, because global capitalism functions effectively like Roman rule in a bygone age. "Religion today allies itself with tele-technoscience, to which it reacts with all its forces. It *is*, on the one hand, globalization; it produces, weds, exploits the capital and knowledge of tele-mediatization; neither the trips and global spectacularization of the Pope, nor the interstate dimensions of the 'Rushdie affair,' nor planetary terrorism would otherwise be possible." Yet religion at the same time is hostile to this technology-driven reorganization of the world. It constitutes an "autoimmune" reaction, whereby instead of protecting the new world "body" from those pathogens that would destroy it, it attacks this very world. It "reacts immediately, simultaneously, declaring war against that which gives it this new power only at the cost of dislodging it from all its proper places, *in truth from place itself*, from the *taking place* of its truth. It conducts a terrible war against that which protects it only by threatening it, according to this double and contradictory structure: immunitary and auto-immunitary."[16] The "return" of religion is actually a resurgence, a violent reaction to the relativizing, historicizing, and "liberating" effects of modernity.

The same point is made, though less technically and philosophically, by Friedman. Friedman acknowledges what Derrida discovered a decade before him. According to Friedman, the "flat world" amounts to a level playing field for all economic parties. But "the playing field is not being leveled only in ways that draw in and superempower a whole new group of innovators. It's being leveled in a

16. Ibid., 82.

way that draws in and superempowers a whole new group of angry, frustrated, and humiliated men and women," such as al-Qaida.[17] Friedman tends to view religious militancy in the way secularist political economists do, as outrage against perceived worldly injustice. Friedman mainly documents what Derrida predicted even before Osama bin Laden launched his first strike against the Khobar Towers in Saudi Arabia in the mid-1990s.

As an article for the prestigious Pew Forum by Timothy Samuel Shah and Monica Duffy Toft put the matter, it is not clear that those who tout the familiar globalist, or "globalatinist," model of a world made safe from upheaval by the economic pacification of the religious impulse have really "gotten it." The caption for the article makes an observation that anyone who has closely followed global politics and trends in at least the past decade could easily make, but which has often been resisted by the culture of the secular news media. "Religion was supposed to fade away as [secular] democracy spread. Instead, it's booming around the world—and often deciding who gets elected."[18] As part of a string of factoids, the article goes on to report that "the period in which economic and political modernization has been most intense—the last 30 to 40 years—has witnessed a jump in religious vitality around the world." Christianity and Islam, the planet's two largest faith communities, have expanded at a rate exceeding population growth. According to the article, the trend toward religious growth has been deepened by an explosion of new constituencies "with traditional religious views."[19] Shah and Toft dismiss the common view that these traditionalist movements are some sort of "return to the Middle Ages," as the conventional wisdom goes. Instead, "today's religious upsurge" can be explained more as "an explosion of 'neo-orthodoxies.'"

The spread of religion has proceeded in tandem also with a more aggressive effort on the part of local groups to bring their faith and values into the public arena. Such neo-orthodoxies (not to be confused with the well-known brand of Christian theology that flourished in the United States and Europe from the 1920s through the early 1960s) utilize sophisticated communications technology

17. Friedman, *The World Is Flat*, 8.
18. Timothy Samuel Shah and Monica Duffy Toft, "God Is Winning," *Dallas Morning News*, July 16, 2006, 1P.
19. Ibid., 4P.

and organizational and fund-raising techniques that come with the present social and economic territory. Shah and Toft conclude: "The belief that outbreaks of politicized religion are temporary detours on the road to secularization was plausible in 1976, 1986, or even 1996. Today, the argument is untenable. As a framework for explaining and predicting the course of global politics, secularism is increasingly unsound."[20]

If in the battle with secularism "God is winning," as the title of the article phrases it, what does that really mean concretely, and what implications does it have for global Christianity, particularly evangelical Christianity, which far more than Roman Catholicism has brought the majority of new believers into its fold? Shah and Toft lead off their article by citing the victory of Hamas in the last Palestinian election and give considerable attention to the rise of Islamism in the Muslim world. Obviously what is happening in the Muslim sphere, where a profound antipathy toward modern secularism has been a deep current throughout the modernization of the Middle East, is only superficially symmetrical with what has been happening with Christianity in Asia, Africa, and Latin America. Because secularism has always been identified in the Muslim mind with encroachments from the West—in the view of Islamists with a defilement of the sacred and historical unity of the *Dar al-Islam* (House of Submission), of Muslim political and spiritual unity—the "return of religion" in that realm is less surprising, even though its militancy, single-mindedness, and virulence continues to astound casual Western analysts.

The Era of Disenchantment

The demise of the secular ironically did not begin in the developing world, but in secular America itself more than three decades ago. Americans have short historical memory. But we should recall that the death-of-God movement in the mid-1960s, featured in a famous special edition of *Time* magazine in 1965 that marked the high-water point of secularist sentiment in this country, was quickly followed by the cultural fallout from the disastrous Vietnam War and the acceleration of violence and social breakdown during the second half of that decade. America's era of disenchantment reached

20. Ibid., 5P.

its peak with the Watergate scandals, Arab oil embargoes, runaway inflation, and President Carter's politically controversial speech about American "malaise" during the 1970s. This era corresponded to a deep-reaching revival of spirituality in new and unprecedented forms throughout America and to a lesser extent in Western Europe. Everything from the advent of the Jesus movement in California to the new charismatics in Anglo-Catholicism to the proliferation of strange cults to the emergence of what in the 1980s became known as the New Age phenomenon can be cataloged as key components of this trend. Commentators at the time frequently referred to these changes, perhaps a bit ambiguously, as a "third great awakening," comparing them to the waves of religious enthusiasm engulfing America in the 1740s and 1820s. In retrospect much of this shift, especially when it came to what in the 1970s had been termed the "Asian invasion" of gurus and Eastern meditation practices, could be attributed to a "reverse globalization" of sorts.

The contemporary paradigm of globalization presupposes that it is something emanating principally from the West, or that it is at least a caravan for the transport of Western values, institutions, and technologies. To critics of globalization, the process is often dismissed as a kind of neocolonialism. But the initial beachhead against secularism was made by "missionaries" from the East, mainly spiritual leaders or monks from India, Japan, Korea, or Tibet who found a promising market for their teachings, writings, and prescriptions for religious discipline among young, disgruntled baby boomers. These traders in what previously had been perceived to be exotic religious commodities began penetrating the American market in the mid-1960s as their standing in their own home cultures, undergoing rapid modernization, had taken a tumble. The Maharishi Mahesh Yogi, who founded Transcendental Meditation and won an instant following because of his role as spiritual adviser to the Beatles, made the greatest splash during that period. He was followed by the Hare Krishna devotees, the Guru Maharaj Ji, the Rev. Sun Myung Moon, Bhagwan Rajneesh, and many other renowned or notorious leaders of what were first called "new religions" and later the New Age movement. It would not be an exaggeration to say that the resurgence of religion worldwide had its genesis in this setting, although the first glimmerings of the Islamist revolt against secular Arab regimes can also be traced to this period as well. The Islamic upsurge was due largely to the growing influence of the Islamic Brotherhood—which reputedly engineered the assassination of Egyptian President Anwar Sadat in 1981—and to the long-term fallout from the Iranian Islamic Revolution, which overthrew the shah in 1979.

The new evangelicalism broadly termed "postmodern" these days was seeded during this American religious revival, which ironically rejected mainstream Protestantism. The same acids of postmodernity dissolved the influence of Protestant denominationalism all across the theological spectrum and initially gave rise to the "postdenominational" megachurch—a term popularized by Fuller Seminary professor Peter Wagner—and the meteoric impact of the new television megaministries. The present emerging church movement was a delayed reaction to these 1980ish styles of mega-evangelicalism, but the causes were also quite similar. The postmodernizing of world Christianity had its precursors in the demodernizing of American religion, which can be seen as a sort of nativist spiritual revolt of the postwar generation against a highly rationalized and bureaucratic Protestantism. It is no accident that the 1960s hippies made a romantic fetish out of American Indians and earth-based spirituality. The cultural upheaval in America throughout the 1960s and 1970s provided something of a template for what would happen in the developing world, so far as global Christianity is concerned.

Global Postmodern Christianity

There are three essential characteristics of what we must recognize as global postmodern Christianity: decentralization, deinstitutionalization, and indigenization. We know what is connoted by the first two terms, but what precisely is implied by the third? By "indigenization" we mean a process by which—if we read closely the philosophical arguments of Deleuze—universal concepts are intelligible only if they are understood in light of specific circumstances. In fact, Deleuze insists that the basic notion of universally valid "scientific" concepts, as ensconced in Greek philosophy and so ingrained in the thought habits of the modern West, distorts the underlying laws of language and meaning by which people actually communicate and agree with one another. According to Deleuze, meaning or signification is located in the singularity of an event. The event, which as a singularity always has a particular location in time and space, generates other comparable or connected events down the line. And the chain of these events, when viewed retrospectively, crystallizes as a concept.

Even broad and abstract concepts, mainly philosophical ones, have both a genealogy and an ordered arrangement across the span of history. They are comparable to what in contemporary mathematics are known as fractals—forms or structures that are built by the process of recursion. The Merriam-Webster online dictionary defines "recursion" as "the determination of a succession of elements (as numbers or functions) by operation on one or more preceding elements according to a rule or formula involving a finite number of steps." Snowflakes are fractals, which makes them infinitely varied, as human observers have discerned for centuries.

But each snowflake is generated by a rule of recursion starting with the shape of the original particle. This notion of the concept as a kind of historically determined fractal, as opposed to the standard classical and Enlightenment definition of it as a logically self-similar idea that persists without variation across the ages, is not merely a strange, postmodernist innovation in thought that abandons us in the shadowlands of irrationality. It also is the key to so much of current advanced science, not just fractal geometry, which is used extensively by geographers and crystallographers, but also to chaos theory and complexity theory, employed for sophisticated weather forecasting and geology.

The principle that defines these contemporary scientific procedures that rely on the mathematics of recursion, in contrast with the older modernist preoccupation with the logic of identity and formal demonstration, is quite straightforward. In modernist thinking the "real is rational," as the philosopher Hegel phrased it, if after being shown in all its countless examples it remains self-same, or identical with itself. In the postmodernist view of things articulated philosophically by Deleuze and applied scientifically through fractal geometry, the real is rational if its numerous iterations are produced by a rule of development that the new mathematics terms "self-similarity."

The real as a universal truth or object instantiated in a concrete situation, or sequence of situations, does not have to be the same as itself. It only has to bear some similarity to itself as it takes on a life of its own. Furthermore, the similarity or likeness is measured by the relationship between the thing in its distinctive circumstances and moment and its immediate progeny, or replication. Thus a child resembles his or her parents, but a similarity between an ancestor and someone in the fifteenth generation down the line may be gauged only by analyzing one's genetic makeup.

The twentieth-century philosopher Ludwig Wittgenstein, who invented linguistic analysis, or analytic philosophy, provided an insight into this problem when, by resorting to the more traditional philosophical approach coming from the Enlightenment, he tried to identify the connection between certain logical propositions, which were supposed to embody what the eighteenth century had called the "pure concept." He realized at once that they were not the same, only similar. Did the lack of identity, only the presence of similarity, defeat the purpose of logic, as far as Wittgenstein was concerned? Not at all. He fell back on the illustration of what one sees when one looks at a family picture that offers a comparison of the physical features of not only parents and children but also of siblings, grandparents, aunts, uncles, and cousins. In peering at the family album, Wittgenstein noted, one can never find a common property that distinguishes everyone in the picture. But one can find a web of family resemblances that are recognizable yet not reducible to a single factor. One "knows" that these people all are descended from the same genetic stock, but one cannot necessarily stipulate what they all have exactly in common.

Nor can one define exactly what that genetic stock actually is. But we know that whatever it is, that stock is somehow incarnate in, or indigenized through, the singular person who shares it. Throughout his later work Deleuze invoked the botanical category of the rhizome to help explicate this pattern of change. The word itself is derived from a Greek compound that means a "mass of roots." Rhizomes are always subterranean and promote growth without seeing the light of day. Unlike a tuber, such as a potato, which decays as it sends up shoots into the atmosphere and sends down roots into the soil before it replicates itself below, a rhizome sustains itself and spreads horizontally, often thickening with nourishment for further growth. Rhizomes can engender both roots and shoots simultaneously without ever dissipating. Deleuze contrasts rhizomic growth with what he calls the "arboreal" (after the trajectory of tree growth). Rhizomic growth is global rather than local; it is basically invisible and can manifest in different ways in different places.

Deleuze's discovery that a concept can only be construed fractally, genealogically, indigenously, or rhizomically has tremendous implications for grasping what is going on with the new postmodern

GloboChristianity. Westerners cling to the outmoded modernist assumption that Christianity is basically the same, or should be the same, everywhere in the world; it is easy for us to miss what exactly is the latest third-millennium installment of worldwide efforts to fulfill the Great Commission. Because the Western Christianity we know has for years been slowly dying, or at least sputtering, we are wont to suppose that the faith as a whole is in its terminal stages.

But for the past several decades now, data from missions organizations and demographic surveys have showed a rapid expansion in the practices and influence of Christianity beyond the West, even among those segments of the world population where other religious traditions have dominated in the past. Nor can the explosive growth of GloboChristianity be attributed mainly to the legacy of European hegemony and colonialism, which has been fast on the wane while indigenous forms of the church are taking over. On a global scale Christianity looks less and less like what is taught in historical or Western sociological textbooks.

In his provocative book *Whose Religion Is Christianity? The Gospel beyond the West*, Lamin Sanneh, professor of missions and world Christianity at Yale Divinity School, argues that globalization and indigenization has brought about a remarkable rebirth of an ancient faith analogous more to what happened during the first three centuries of the Roman Empire than to what took place even after the three hundred years that followed the Protestant Reformation. As far as global Christianity is concerned, we are not witnessing a reformation so much as a transformation. Just as the Jewish Christianity of the initial disciples morphed radically and dramatically after Saul of Tarsus had completed his mission to the gentiles and the temple at Jerusalem had been razed by Roman legions, so world Christianity is undergoing a total overhaul now that Europe has become secular, America is engulfed in its own parochial culture wars, and Westernization has been replaced by indigenization—the religious version of the world-is-flat hypothesis.

According to Sanneh,

> The contemporary confidence in the secular destiny of the West as an elevated stage of human civilization is matched by the contrasting evidence of the resurgence of Christianity as a world religion; they are like two streams flowing in opposite directions. Perhaps the two currents have more in common than meets the eye, as if the impetus

of secularization is set to fill the void from which religion has been drained, while religious resurgence elsewhere makes headway in societies not yet captured by secularism. No matter. What is at issue now is the surprising scale and depth of the worldwide Christian resurgence, a resurgence that seems to proceed without Western organizational structures, including academic recognition, and is occurring amid widespread political instability and the collapse of public institutions, part of what it means to speak of a post-Western Christianity. Even church leaders have been unable to comprehend fully, still less to respond effectively to, the magnitude of the resurgence.[21]

Sanneh points out that in Africa in 1910, after the continent had been groaning under the spiked heel of colonialism, only nine percent of the total populace of 108 million was Christian. Many of these Christians had been so for centuries, belonging to the Coptic and Ethiopian Orthodox branches of the church. The percentage was still far less than half in the early 1960s, when colonialism came to an end.

By the mid-1980s, however, Christianity had emerged as the majority religion, and the conversion rate was staggering—almost six million per year.[22] Yet another trend "little noticed in the statistics," Sanneh says, "is a theological one: Christian expansion was virtually limited to those societies whose people had preserved the indigenous name for God. That was a surprising discovery, because of the general feeling that Christianity was incompatible with indigenous ideas of religion."[23] In other words, indigenization in Africa has followed the pattern of Catholicism in the ancient Mediterranean and in the northern Europe of the Middle Ages. Local "pagan" forms of worship and religious discourse are also transformed into expressions consonant with the gospel itself.

The primary force driving Christian global expansion—not just in Africa but elsewhere—is neither Westernization nor the economic engines of globalization. It is the rhizomic as well as relational power

21. Lamin Sanneh, *Whose Religion Is Christianity? The Gospel beyond the West* (Grand Rapids: Eerdmans, 2003), 3. See also Lamin Sanneh and Joel A. Carpenter, *The Changing Face of Christianity: Africa, the West, and the World* (New York: Oxford University Press, 2004). A similar argument is offered by Peter Beyer, "De-Centering Religious Singularity: The Globalization of Christianity as a Case in Point," *Numen* 50 (2003): 357–86.
22. Sanneh, *Whose Religion*, 14–15.
23. Ibid., 18.

of the gospel, which, though it cannot be theologically codified in one language or culture, turns them inside out. "World Christianity is not merely an echo of [economic] globalization. On the contrary, in some instances new Christian movements are a reaction to the ravages and threats of globalization, with concerted attention to the value of local cultures and economies, the challenges of social dislocation and marginalization, the interests and dignity of families, and the importance of community well-being. World Christianity is evidence of a boundary-free global economy being witness to boundary-hinged communities of faith."[24]

The rhizomic and relational power of the gospel is evidenced in the overseas work of David Wahlstedt, lead pastor at Crosspointe Community Church in Carrollton, Texas. A graphic designer before entering the ministry, as well as a protégé of famed postmodern ministry theoretician Leonard Sweet of Drew University, Wahlstedt has turned a traditional Reformed congregation with denominational identity and modest financial backing from the Evangelical Presbyterian Church (EPC) into a small but dynamic community-outreach-oriented ministry in the northwestern suburbs of Dallas. But for Wahlstedt, outreach and becoming involved missionally goes far beyond partnering with the Christian social service organizations and other familiar ministries—even the trendy ones—that seek to reach an increasingly ethnically mixed and generationally segregated expanse in one of America's fastest growing metroplexes. It means reaching across oceans to Africa's teeming and impoverished populations that are hungry for the gospel, however they can gain access to it. Crosspointe does not merely send or support missionaries who annually or semi-annually make a brief home visit and stand before the congregation to report on how "God is working" far from the experience of the average suburban professional and their families. Wahlstedt goes once a year to Uganda and stands in for his own congregation, building relationships as well as a constant cross-flow of stories and information between the two vastly different worlds. Because Crosspointe is not, and does not intend to become, a mega-church, the communities on either side of the ocean have their own sense of investment in and relationship with each other.

The Uganda Children's Project (UCP), as it is called, was conceived in 2001 after a Ugandan nurse visited the church where Wahlstedt

24. Ibid., 75.

was serving in Chattanooga, Tennessee. She shared with Wahlstedt that her brother-in-law had passed away and that his children would now be living with her and her husband. Her biggest concern was how she and her husband would be able to provide an education for these children. She went on to explain that although there is a free public education system throughout Uganda, there are costs associated with attendance that each family must absorb. Her family's meager income would not be sufficient to pay the extra costs to have these children attend school. An elder at the church in Tennessee agreed to sponsor the children. Within a few weeks the elder learned of fourteen more children with desperate need of sponsorship. He found sponsors for those children, and the project was born. Today, over 325 children are sponsored by members of local churches across the Southeast and in Texas.[25]

Wahlstedt's own involvement grew as the number of children in the project continued to increase. Within a year of its inception there were four Ugandan nationals administering the project. The elder mentioned above invited Wahlstedt to join him on a trip to Kampala during the summer of 2002. Wahlstedt has been going back ever since. He and the same elder travel while raising funds and sponsorships for the nearly four hundred children still on a waiting list for entrance into the project. Funds are sought predominately through the EPC and personal connections.

Wahlstedt brought both his passion for Uganda generally and the project specifically when he assumed the lead pastor role at Crosspointe. "Our people caught the vision for partnering with this mission immediately," he writes. Crosspointe is a "huge part" of the project insofar as they contribute financially "but in other tangible ways as well." He adds: "without the support of the church leadership, I would be unable to take time away from my pastoral duties to raise funds and travel yearly" to Uganda. "None of the time I spend working with the UCP is counted against my vacation or off days." The UCP "fits beautifully into our missions strategy. Our goal is to be involved in strategic mission partnerships locally, nationally and internationally." At Crosspointe "mission" and "missional" converge. UCP is tied closely to the vision of Crosspointe, which triangulates it both with a growing partnership with Christian

25. The Web site for the project can be found at (www.ugandachildrensproject .org).

Community Action—a thirty-year-old ministry that serves the poor through a food pantry, resale shop, vocational training, and community health services—and its own church plant in Los Angeles.[26]

UCP, Wahlstedt says, "has been a part of my church's missional DNA from the day I arrived." It is distinctive from other overseas missions because of the "personal nature of the relationships between sponsored child and sponsor." The relationship between child and sponsor is paternal and fraternal in many ways. "Many of these children are orphans and look upon their sponsors as parents." Regular letter and video messages are shared and sponsors receive their child's report card each semester. Many of the sponsors have visited Uganda during one of the church's twice-yearly trips. Only a very small percentage of funds raised go toward administrative costs with the lion's share going to the children themselves. Everyone picks up their own expenses. The motto of UCP is "changing Uganda one child at a time," which means that change itself is relational and the relationship among the different churches is networked, or "rhizomic."[27]

If global Christianity is a God-directed cry among the distress of those uprooted and displaced by the economies of globalization, on the spiritual side it is meeting fierce resistance as well. The world may appear flat these days in terms of investment flows and the exchange of goods and services, but dark clouds are beginning to roil and roll across the fruited plain of technology-generated prosperity. If Christianity is resurgent as a global faith force, so is the new globalized Islam. Islam's resurgence is due to the same rhizomic tendencies that we find in Christianity, though the outcome is obviously quite different. What is the meaning of this dual resurgence that offers the possibility of a worldwide battle of the titans for the spiritual future of the planet? We will address this prospect in chapter 4, but first we must understand better what is signified when we say Christianity is becoming a GloboChristianity. We must understand that GloboChristianity, a globopomo Christianity, is first and foremost an incarnational Christianity in which missions and the missional are seamlessly interwoven.

26. Telephone conversation with David Wahlstedt, December 31, 2007.
27. Ibid.

2

De-Signs of the Time

> I see Christ as the incarnation of the piper who is calling us. He dances that shape and pattern which is at the heart of our reality.
>
> Sydney Carter

The Incarnational Christian

The secret of Christianity's growth throughout the ages has always been its unstinting push to evangelize non-Christian peoples and cultures. Contrary to politically correct thinking prevalent nowadays throughout the secular West, this impulse does not emerge from some lingering imperial drive of one civilization to dominate the other or even of one religion to dominate over all the others. It originates in Jesus's explicit instructions to his followers, which tradition has named "the Great Commission."

The key passage is found at the conclusion of the Gospel of Matthew. "The eleven disciples made their way to Galilee, to the mountain where Jesus had told them to meet. When they saw him, they fell prostrate before him, though some were doubtful. Jesus then came up and spoke to them. He said: 'Full authority in heaven and on earth has been committed to me. Go forth therefore and make all nations my disciples; baptize . . . [people] everywhere in the name of the Father and the Son and the Holy Spirit, and teach

47

them to observe all that I have commanded you. And be assured, I am with you always, to the end of time'" (Matt. 28:16–20 NEB).

The Great Commission, as many close readers of the Gospel text itself have emphasized, is not really about getting the message out. It is not, as hucksters have tended to spin it, simply about market-ing the distinctive name brand we call Christianity from Toronto to Timbuktu in much the same way that fast-food or consumer com-modities are promoted and sold in a variety of different cultures. It is not about planting churches wherever one can from Hindustan to the Netherlands. It is about manifesting and making real the mean-ing of the paradox of the incarnation and the miracle of Christ's resurrection.

The operative phrase is contained in the sentence: *egō meth' hymōn eimi pasas tas hēmeras*, "I am with you always." The verse harks back to Jesus's oft-cited saying in Matthew 18:20 ("Where two or three have met together in my name, I am there among them" [NEB]) as well as to Matthew 1:23, where the angel announces to Mary that her son will fulfill the Emmanuel prophecy of Isaiah, that Jesus will be "God with us." The Great Commission, when all is said and done, rests upon the great postmodern preposition—the "with" of divine relation as contrasted with the "is" of doctrinal propositions. God is never what he is "in himself." God is always *mit uns* (with us) or *für uns* (for us), as Luther insisted. He is what he is *in relation to us*. The Great Commission, which Jesus pronounced at the same loca-tion where he delivered the Sermon on the Mount, transforms the Christian faith into something that is much more than a new torah, or instruction, from on high. It is not divine revelation so much as it is divine relation, a relationship that is "with us always." It is a relation that must be propagated until the "end of time."

The incarnation, God becoming man, is the beachhead for this never-flagging relationship. All ministry must be incarnational in this sense, as authors Michael Frost and Alan Hirsch have pleaded. As their slogan goes, "the missional church is incarnational."[1] The church must be the bearer not just of good tidings but also of inti-mate confidings. It must be made present not just in local situations but also in the sensitive space of people's daily lives. Obviously the world today, though, is vastly different than it was in Jesus's day.

---

1. Michael Frost and Alan Hirsch, *The Shaping of Things to Come: Innovation and Mission for the 21st-Century Church* (Peabody, MA: Hendrickson, 2003), 43.

History has taken a postmodern turn, whatever that implies. Has the Great Commission taken a postmodern turn as well? In what direction are we now led?

What did Jesus have in mind when he commissioned those of us who are Christ-followers to "go forth" and "make all nations my disciples"? This injunction has been construed, usually by evangelicals, as implying that one must journey abroad and witness to some remote, strange, or lost peoples at the margins of civilization and bring them into the fold of some foggily conceived world spiritual community once known as Christendom. Sending high school and college students to Mexico, Costa Rica, or even Japan or the Congo on a mission trip during their summer vacations is a time-honored and cliché-encrusted method of "fulfilling" the commission. But is that really what Jesus envisioned? The mission trip survives as the churchy counterpart to the grand tour of Europe on which modern parents of proper income and rank dispatched their children so that they might experience the world before settling into the burdens and responsibilities of adulthood.

The Greek phrase *panta ta ethnē* (all nations) has the force of the Hebrew *gôyîm*, which is usually translated as "the gentiles," or "non-Jews," those who are aliens as far as Jews are concerned. It does not primarily mean "other countries," even those countries that have not been converted to Christianity. In the Jewish context "the nations" connoted spiritual and moral inferiority, and we must remember that Jesus spoke thoroughly as a Jew. But what makes the Great Commission distinctive is that Jesus preached, and Paul taught, that the gentiles would be the ones to receive the good news of the risen Messiah in this new era, or dispensation. The message of Emmanuel, "God with us," would be rejected largely by those for whom it should have been evident and familiar, but it would be embraced by those who from the Jewish—and by extension what in the present day we would dub the "religious"—point of view were the feared, inferior, or suspect Others. Therefore the demand that we make pupils or "instruct" (from the Greek verb *mathēteuō*) "all nations" really implies that one reach out *as a priority* to those who are completely different from oneself. Those Others who are wholly other can be ensconced right in one's own near environs or in some remote ultima Thule.

How does a Christian bent on discipling approach and speak to the Other in this sense? What does it really suggest to go at things in an incarnational manner and to live out the Great Commission spiritually as well as literally? Frost and Hirsch have a surprising answer. Just as normal business advice offered to would-be restaurant owners can be summed up as "location, location, location," so the loud exhortation we should offer ministries that want to be missional in more than name is as follows: contextualize, contextualize, contextualize! According to Frost and Hirsch, "It might seem obvious . . . that if the church is prepared to adopt an incarnational stance, it should take seriously the issue of contextualization."[2]

Contextualization is not some postmodern heresy, as many old-school evangelicals often complain, because it was the gist of everything Jesus himself did. Jesus's lifestyle "was marked by his preferential involvement in the lives of ordinary people, rather than pious religious people. He partied with Matthew and his friends; he played with children; he fried fish for breakfast with Peter; he provided wine for a wedding in Cana." The first Christians also had no choice but to practice contextualization. "Any study of the preaching styles and content of the sermons in Acts will reveal that the gospel message was presented in differing ways depending on whom it was presented to."[3]

For Jews, effective preaching always cited Old Testament prophecies. It is well known that the earliest Christian converts were Jews. These Jews lived mainly outside Jerusalem and in a Dispersion, or Diaspora, throughout the Mediterranean. During the first century and for a while after that, Christianity was largely, if not exclusively, Jewish in its outlook. When Paul took his mission to Athens, however, he contextualized his message in the idiom of Greek philosophy and even backed his argument with a well-known quote from a Hellenistic poet.[4] At the Areopagus, which was both an intellectual and legal center of Greek life, Paul did not insist on haranguing with Jewish Scripture, which the Greeks would have considered to be an offensive rhetorical technique peculiar to an exotic, Eastern cult.

The Western church in general, and the American evangelical church specifically, has made such a fetish out of its own rigidly modernistic, though admittedly diverse, forms of "Christian" culture that it does not realize that it has been contextualizing all along.

2. Ibid., 84.
3. Ibid., 85.
4. See Acts 17:16–34.

"When churches in the West talk about contextualization, they are often meaning nothing more than a simple change in the style of music or the introduction of drums or new seating to replace the pews."[5] Even the so-called emerging church movement, which has incorporated the postmodern principles of de-institutionalization and horizontal organization while stressing relational types of ministry, falls short in this regard. By some measures the emerging church has stumbled into a less-apparent modernistic snare of its own making by becoming increasingly identified with American or European youth culture, all the while constantly striving, at least in terms of its most visible leadership, to be hipper than thou without paying serious attention to the deeper and more intractable cries of the planet's downtrodden and lost.

By some estimates the emerging church is simply reenacting the fateful missteps of mainline Protestantism in the late 1960s and early 1970s, when it was challenged by the radical secularists of the time and absorbed the influences of the youth-based counterculture, which took root on the West Coast and spread across the country on the tide of general revulsion at the war in Vietnam. It did radically contextualize and succeeded in remaining relevant for a while.

The word "relevant," as veterans of the 1960s counterculture like myself are old enough to remember, is a well-worn mantra that has been taken up again as a watchword by emerging Christians, yet with little historical consciousness of what went on a generation or more ago. But within twenty years the Christian counterculture had basically given up on allowing the power of the gospel to transform personal lives as well as entirely new cultures and circumstances. This movement had become simply one segment of the middle-class culture defined and embraced by graying baby boomers—what columnist David Brooks in the 1990s wryly labeled "bobo [bohemian bourgeois] culture."[6] Mainstream Protestant Christians were now more intellectually and culturally sophisticated as well as more politically liberal, but they had little use for Christianity with its deeper spiritual challenges and demands on our moral life. The mainline churches became liberal. They were preoccupied with social issues rather than with questions of the heart. When those social issues

5. Frost and Hirsch, *The Shaping of Things to Come*, 85.
6. See David Brooks, *Bobos in Paradise: The New Upper Class and How They Got There* (New York: Simon & Schuster, 2001).

seemed less compelling or relevant, the mainline churches rapidly
faded from the picture.

Relevance in a Global Context

But relevance is, paradoxically, also a virtue that we by necessity must cultivate if we are to remain faithful to what Jesus commanded us. Jesus certainly was thoroughly relevant to his day and
age, although often in a different way than the term is frequently
intended. Jesus was relevant in the sense that he was always willing,
prepared, and committed to going where the Spirit of God drove
him or where his Father was calling him. Jesus was bent on bearing
any burden or paying any price to do what needed to be done at
that particular moment in time, in that distinct place, or in response
to that specific challenge or situation. It is a staple of dogma to
connect the idea of incarnation to Jesus's death and resurrection
on the cross. But we must recognize that Jesus anticipated this
event—in other words, he was already incarnational—throughout
the scope of his earthly ministry. Jesus launched his ministry with
a proclamation that the "kingdom of God" was "near" or had
"approached" (Greek: *ēngiken*).[7] The form derives from the Greek
verb *engizō*, which has the force of something inevitably drawing near, of becoming intimately present in either time or space.
But it is not merely about something or someone coming a little
closer, so that earlier arrangements or relations are not seriously
disrupted. It is about the distant suddenly becoming proximate or,
as we say theologically, of experiencing the transcendent all at once
as immanent. The unexpected arrival of what Jesus announced—
the kingdom of God, *basileia tou theou*—coincided with his own
appearance and peregrinations. Jesus became relevant because he
manifested God's awesome power and presence, which remained
for a time ambiguous and invisible to the eyes of unbelievers, at
moments and sites where previously it had merely been the "same
old, same old." Relevance meant a revolutionary relationality of
God to his creation that burst like a thunderclap on the landscape
of a secular world.

7. Mark 1:15. Older English versions of the New Testament frequently translate
the phrase as "at hand."

Those thunderclaps are sounding across previously parched deserts. *Relevant* magazine, familiar for many years to readers as largely an appendage of the Christian rock industry and the urban youth ministry scene, has started to become more relevant in this broader global sense. Fred Wright, a minister from the Bell Creek Community Church in metro Detroit, describes in *Relevant* his expedition to Zambia to instruct new Christian pastors in the African bush on how to read and teach the Bible. "Spiritually, it's about 37 AD," Wright exclaims, "right out of the book of Acts. The gospel has taken root, but the roots don't go too deep yet." The comment out of context may sound slightly paternalistic, but that is not Wright's aim in the article. Instead, he strives to make the point that even though his initial experience of "terror" in driving fast over rutted-out dirt roads into the middle of nowhere to reach the remote African village where he is working hurled him rudely out of his Western Christian comfort zone, he has received a valuable lesson in what the Great Commission truly means. It is all about incarnational ministry. "'Incarnation' is a funky word," Wright says. "We don't use it much unless we're talking theology, but we need to get it back into our vocabulary." The Western church, he adds, has become obsessed with missions professionalism, "the view that missions is best left to highly trained, highly called, special-force type Christians who will go out there and save the world." Wright suggests that this attitude has provided missionaries with a persistent rationale *not* to reach the rural hinterlands of the global South, where a thirst for the gospel is immense. He tells how throughout his visit the back-country pastors expressed their amazement that a white man would even bother to visit them. "As I get ready to leave, some have tears in their eyes and say that my presence is evidence that God loves them and has heard their cries. Whoa. But that's what incarnational ministry does. When we go to a hard place, humble ourselves, and live with the people we want to minister to, it echoes the nature of Jesus, who did the same for us." Incarnational ministry is recognized by the fact that we allow God to work through our persons, not our credentials, titles, organizations, not even our trendiness. "Pick a place, a people," Wright concludes, "and glorify the Triune God who is invisible but powerfully present by being there."[8]

8. Fred Wright, "Incarnational Ministry," *Relevant* (November 2005), http://www.relevantmagazine.com/god_article.php?id=7016.

Even Brian McLaren, the most well-known postmodern Christian leader, whom *Time* magazine a few years ago named one of
the twenty-five most influential evangelicals in America, has recently
been sounding the same theme. In early 2007 McLaren was invited
to Africa for a global meeting of leaders of emerging churches.
"We were black, white, colored . . . from the U.S., Canada, Sweden,
Switzerland, Korea, Australia, Liberia, Dominican Republic, Costa
Rica, and South Africa," McLaren writes. "We met in Mokona,
Uganda, just north of Kampala, and then divided into teams to visit
churches and leaders in rural Uganda, Rwanda, and Kenya before
returning to debrief and share our experiences. We represented 'the
church that is emerging'—emerging from the colonial mind-set, the
modern mind-set, the nationalist mentality, the denominational and
sectarian assumptions, the old polarities of left and right, liberal
and conservative. We came together for dialogue around the gospel
of Jesus Christ."[9]

McLaren contrasts the emerging church with the prosperity gospel, which has taken over certain strains of Pentecostalism and has
spread its viny tendrils throughout the impoverished villages of the
global South. Prosperity Christianity is all the rage because it speaks
to immediate needs: "My God never lets me go a day without lunch,"
R. Andrew Chestnut, who has studied Pentecostal prosperity fervor
throughout Latin America, quotes one follower as confessing.[10] But
McLaren suggests that what makes the kind of Christianity he represents both relevant and real is that he is reaching out to suffering
but hopeful Christ-followers. McLaren says he speaks for churches
that are "living out a transformational, incarnational, integral gospel around the world" and not just pushing snake oil. A woman to
whom he gives this assurance seems a little dubious, according to
his account. It is not clear to what degree incarnational ministry, or
contextualism, in this instance would entail addressing her abject
poverty in a very concrete manner.

In an e-mail to his Emergent Village readers dated April 26, 2007,
McLaren asserts: "I have become convinced of two things in this travel.
First, we Christians in the West or North (and especially in the United

9. Brian McLaren, "Reflections on Amahoro-Africa May 2007," http://www.brian
mclaren.net/archives/news/reflections-on-amahoroafrica-may.html.
10. R. Andrew Chestnut, *Born Again in Brazil* (New Brunswick, NJ: Rutgers University Press, 1997), 174.

States) live in an echo chamber; it's so hard for us to hear 'the voice of the Other' over the clamor of our own incessant and redundant broadcasting. Second, we desperately need to hear these voices, for our own good and for the potential of increased partnership in the future."[11] Contextualization is ultimately about listening and setting aside our assumptions about what others need—or what we think they need—even if what we think has solid theological underpinnings.

One of the problems contextualizers face is how to do so; the New Testament itself poses the dilemma of being in the world without being of the world. Or the question can be submitted as the renowned Yale theologian H. Richard Niebuhr did a half century ago: How can we be equipped so that Christ becomes the "transformer" of culture without ending up being the "Christ *of* culture"? A Christ *of* culture is simply an image shaped from all the predilections and prejudices of the age. Yet the question today runs even deeper than Niebuhr originally cast it. McLaren himself raises this question, though he does not seem to have a satisfactory answer on the spot. With the changes rapidly taking place in our very Western epistemology because of globalization and relentless intercultural borrowings and transactions, we may ask: How do we maintain the integrity of our confession as Christians? How do we indigenize without relativizing? What is the authentic import of the scriptural proclamation that "Jesus Christ is the same yesterday and today and forever" (Heb. 13:8)?

McLaren cites a brief essay by Sherman YL Kuek, OSL, "an itinerant minister" and adjunct lecturer in Christian theology at Seminari Theoloji Malaysia. Kuek blogs frequently on the cultural contextualization of the gospel, particularly in Asia, and argues that the historical Roman and Germanic epistemologies that inform so much of Western theology just will not work for Asia. Contextual theology in this sense has certainly been a staple of Asian Christian discourse since at least the sixteenth century, although it is only now in the postcolonial era, with the rising sense in the West of a genuinely global Christianity, that such an approach has been gaining attention outside certain indigenous communities. As the editors of a major resource guide on Asian Christian theologies write, "The thought patterns, the terminology, and the interpretative principles used in incarnational Asian theologies are frequently markedly different from those often assumed to be normative in some other regions.

11. Brian McLaren, *Emergent Village Newsletter*, April 26, 2007.

The systematic metaphysical construction that emerged in the post-medieval West, for example, has seldom been an indispensable—or even recognized—element in incarnational Asian theologies."[12] Asian thought has historically been iconographic and fluid—what we might loosely characterize as the ancient postmodern—rather than the metaphysical. Kuek inquires whether the project of contextualization is ultimately about embellishing a "static universal core" of the gospel, a "series of articulations which is time insensitive and perennially unchanging"—or whether it comes down to enunciating a "dynamic universal core," or "a series of articulations which is time sensitive and perennially changing with the development of our theological understanding." The latter, he says, "is probably the only way by which one can be authentically contextual" in theology. Kuek argues that a global postmodern Christianity is about affirming this "dynamic core" as opposed to "permitting the culture to redefine the core." Culture plays the role of an "interrogator" of the gospel, as it has always done. What Kuek terms the "Great Christian Tradition" has resulted from this cumulative process of interrogation, and it "possesses more than a sufficient wealth of wisdom to provide plausible solutions for challenges posed by culture." Contextual thinkers are always out of their own comfort zones when it comes to culture and conventional faith languages. What they have in common is the dynamic core that consists in countless indigenizations of the gospel by sundry historical, linguistic, and representational means in a succession of moments. Every contextualizer knows oneself to be attesting to "a Great Story of which . . . [one] is a part—consisting of multiple voices of wisdom [from those] who have come before . . . and who would be able to infuse wisdom and impart solutions in . . . [one's] endeavour to be a relevant voice within the present scheme of life."[13]

Evangelicalism and the Question of Culture

Even if contextualization has not been on evangelical ministry's radar screen, the question of culture has always been its

12. John C. England et al., *Asian Christian Theologies: A Research Guide to Authors, Movements, Sources*, vol. 2 (Delhi: Indian Society for Promoting Christian Knowledge, 2003), xlvi.

13. *Emergent Village Newsletter*, April 26, 2007.

topmost priority. One of the shibboleths of the new evangelicalism
is "engaging the culture." This phrase frequently implies that the
faithful in years gone by have walled themselves off from wider
cultural practices and trends and established their own ghetto, a
distinctive Christian subculture. If one examines the history of
American evangelicalism in the twentieth century, that conclusion is surely justified. The Scopes Monkey Trial of 1927 was the
turning point in American history that led to the formation of
such a ghetto. When American evangelicals, who once proudly
referred to themselves as "fundamentalists," were publicly humiliated by Scopes's brilliant attorney Clarence Darrow in their
effort to defend the literal truth of Genesis against evolutionary
science, evangelicals became disheartened; history shows that they
quickly beat a broad and sullen retreat into a Christian ghetto.[14]
Fundamentalists established their own schools and seminaries,
not to mention their own churches. At the same time they became
completely disengaged politically.

That tendency reversed itself in the 1970s when evangelicals became politically active for the first time in over half a century, and the
opening salvos of the culture wars were fired off. It was not the puta-
tive breakdown in social morality during the late 1960s that revved up
evangelical activists so much as a succession of landmark Supreme
Court decisions during the same era—specifically Roe v. Wade and
the outlawing of prayer in schools. These court rulings seemed to
put a straitjacket on religious influence in society and stifle the public
profession of Christianity. By its very nature, evangelicalism fosters
a public, if not necessarily an explicitly political, expression of faith.
The sophistication necessary for effective political organization as
well as the rapid urbanization of evangelical Christianity in the late
twentieth century contributed significantly to its cultural engagement, prompting the postmodern shift we are seeing.

Eventually evangelicalism as a whole outgrew fundamentalism,
which began in the late nineteenth century as an intellectual movement geared toward reconciling modern science with the text of
the Bible. But fundamentalism did some shape-shifting during the
Depression Era, when it became a highly fortified Maginot Line
against modern culture itself. Fundamentalists were far too numerous

14. See Edwin S. Gaustad, *Dissent in American Religion*, rev. ed., Chicago History
of American Religion (Chicago: University of Chicago Press, 2006).

and too immersed in American society to sustain any Amish-like
pretense of staying separate or "fleeing from Babylon," as radical
sectarians in the past have characterized their withdrawal from culture. Engaging the culture or becoming incarnational is not really a
major challenge for evangelicals, at least in theory, insofar as their
missionary—or "missional," as we would say these days—impulse
has always overwhelmed their hostility to non-Christian values and
lifestyles.

In fact, becoming incarnational is the overarching factor in the
emergence of GloboChristianity, which was seeded by evangelicals
during the age of imperialism, when the cultural Christians of Christendom were more intent on taking up "the white man's burden"
(Kipling) and were making civilizing a much higher priority than
Christianizing. In his masterful historical and geographical survey
of GloboChristianity, Philip Jenkins describes it thus:

> For all the hypocrisy and the flagrantly self-serving rhetoric of the
> imperial age, the dedication of the missionaries was beyond ques-
> tion. Knowing as they did the extreme dangers from violence and
> tropical disease, it is inconceivable that so many would have been
> prepared to lay down their lives for European commerce alone, and
> many certainly viewed missionary work as a ticket to martyrdom.
> Their numbers and their zeal both grew mightily after each successive
> revival in the West, especially when such an event coincided with a
> spectacular tale of exploration and martyrdom.[15]

The early Western missionaries were entirely missional in the
current sense of the word because, Jenkins stresses, they made "important concessions" to the full-blown diversity of native cultures,
including the most important one that has sparked the explosion
of indigenized churches—the translation of the Bible into local or
regional dialects. Although at present the term *missional* usually
has the peculiar flavor of reaching out to those untouched by, or
indifferent to, the dominant evangelical subculture, its application
is largely a creative adaptation of what we might dub the "evangelical principle"—following Paul Tillich's idea of a "Protestant
principle"—in culture. The evangelical principle, broadly stated, is

---

15. Philip Jenkins, *The Next Christendom: The Coming of Global Christianity*
(New York: Oxford University Press, 2002), 36.

uniquely intertwined with the principle of postmodernization,[16] not to mention globalization. It comes down to the drive, first articulated in the Great Commission, that discipling requires "going where no one has gone before," if we can adapt the old Star Trek motto.

The standard American rendering of the evangelical principle has been to present the gospel as a simple and practical message that can be tailored and customized to sundry audiences with varying interests and expectations, and then hope that this seed will take root in the lives of those who experience it. Sometimes this method takes on the cartoonish dimension of the street preacher or televangelist, which like all stereotypes has some footing in reality. Sometimes it is far more subtle and soft-pedaled for a constituency that instinctively resists hard-sell preaching.

The "seeker-sensitive" style of ministry pioneered a generation back pursued this latter path; frankly, it was fashioned out of a certain type of postindustrial advertising technique road tested by so-called humanistic psychologists and deployed specifically for the churches, all the while downplaying those mass-marketing methodologies that no longer seemed to work. The technique was summarized in the popular marketing slogan of the 1980s: "meeting them at the mirror of their world," or more cynically, "care for 'em, then snare 'em." Evangelical approaches have historically been bound up with the accepted means of oratorical persuasion, a tradition that (in all fairness) is anchored in Scripture itself as well as the ministry of Jesus. Both were trying to disarm opponents and score points with their admirers.

But in an era that is so oversaturated with, and psychologically immune to, even highly sophisticated strategies of persuasion (thanks to the ubiquity of media in our lives), standard evangelism has slammed up against a concrete wall. One of the underlying rules of commercial advertising is not so much to interest people in a particular good or service as it is to get their attention dramatically, to trigger some creative association with the product that makes them turn their heads and opens them to the desired outcome. Sometimes this association is fostered without any kind of wordsmithing or message-crafting at

16. In my last book, *The Next Reformation: Why Evangelicals Must Embrace Postmodernity* (Grand Rapids: Baker Academic, 2004), I argued for the close association between the genuine evangelicalism that goes back to the Protestant Reformation started by Luther in 1517 on one hand, and the opportunities presented by postmodernity on the other.

all. It relies on promoting the vague sense in enough people's worlds that something unusual is happening, which will naturally translate into product interest down the line.

This latest trendy wisdom in the ad business is known simply as *buzz marketing*, which aims to create a buzz and is sometimes launched in an inconspicuous, if not necessarily covert, manner. Starting a buzz is not direct manipulation of people's sensibilities with a certain end in view, as one might reasonably huff, because the agent who starts the buzz is never sure how the process will unfold, as in the familiar game of rumor. The purpose is ultimately to lead those who are at the middle or end of the buzz line to trace it back to its source. Satisfying their curiosity about what is really going on is often enough get them to pay attention to the product or service, if only because it now is part of a nexus of association that has formed in the customer's mind.

At the risk of making evangelism sound like a commercial plot and of perhaps coming across as wholly outlandish, one might venture to argue that Jesus himself made effective use of the buzz. Consider the key story of Jesus in the company of his disciples when Peter for the first time recognizes who his master really is. "When he came to the territory of Caesarea Philippi, Jesus asked his disciples, 'Who do men say that the Son of Man is?' They answered, 'Some say John the Baptist, others Elijah, others Jeremiah, or one of the prophets.' 'And you,' he asked, 'who do you say that I am?' Simon Peter answered: 'You are the Messiah, the Son of the living God.' Then Jesus said: 'Simon son of Jonah, you are favoured indeed! You did not learn that from mortal man; it was revealed to you by my heavenly Father'" (Matt. 16:13–17 NEB).

Now take careful note of what is going on in this passage. Jesus's question to Peter is not a rhetorical or trick question, as if the answer were somehow obvious, but the disciple's obtuseness somehow clouds the picture. As Bible scholars have repeatedly commented, the expression "Son of Man," which according to the Gospels was Jesus's own self-designation, was highly problematic for the average audience of his day. Even today what it meant in Jesus's time remains something of an enigma, though it was identified, as we know, with certain passages from the literature known as apocalyptic. Clearly, Jesus did not choose the title to make it obvious or easy for people to figure out who he was. There were innumerable rumors about him, and Jesus did not try to discourage them. By his own intent or by his knowledge of how people react to an intriguing personage and related situations, Jesus started a buzz. The buzz was amplified by the term he chose to define himself.

At the same time, it is only by a disclosure not given to "mortal man" that Peter is able to translate the mysterious locution "Son of Man" into something that will resonate strongly with everyone concerned, although Peter's surprise answer was not a lucky guess. Jesus is emphatic that if the truth had not been "revealed," Peter could not have sorted it out on his own. The buzz Jesus creates is intended to nurture a general environment within which someone like Peter, who is already intimately attached to Jesus, may be totally receptive to a surprising move of God in one's life. The special relation Jesus has to his disciples is the necessary occasion for someone such as Peter finally to "know" him not just as rabbi, but also as Messiah, and thereby know who God actually is in a way that would soon turn the world upside down.

Until that point Peter was perhaps in awe of Jesus, but for all the wrong reasons. He had a relation to him, but not a genuine God-relation. The relation was not yet incarnational. Peter was familiar with all the religious words like "God," "Messiah," or "salvation." He had been "evangelized" insofar as he, as a Jewish believer, had probably received the message many times over and even accepted it. Like many Jews of his time, he was eagerly awaiting the advent of the Messiah, but he strangely had no inkling that the Messiah was all the while walking and standing right beside him or that this relationship was going to turn out the way it did. The full meaning of the revelation was yet to come.

When we read the succeeding verses, it becomes evident that Peter, although he suddenly realized who Jesus actually was, still somehow didn't get it. "From that time Jesus began to make it clear to his disciples that he had to go to Jerusalem, and there to suffer much from the elders, chief priests, and doctors of the law; to be put to death and to be raised again on the third day. At that Peter took him by the arm and began to rebuke him: 'Heaven forbid!' he said. 'No, Lord, this shall never happen to you.' Then Jesus turned and said to Peter, 'Away with you, Satan; you are a stumbling block to me. You think as men think, not as God thinks'" (Matt. 16:21–23 NEB). Peter could not bring himself to grant that the Messiah would be crucified and that this event was part of God's plan. The notion violated every theological presupposition that he held dear to himself.

So Peter still did not really know Jesus. That would have to await the miracle of Sunday morning following Good Friday. He was still thinking like a human, even though it made eminent sense to think that way. To think "as God thinks" would require the final revelation of Jesus's risen glory. In addition, Jesus does not simply dismiss Peter's lack of comprehension at this point as an understandable failure to solve a baffling riddle. He truly rebukes the presence of Satan in that situation, implying that the way religion—or we would say "church"—normally prompts us to think is a manifestation of the Prince of Darkness himself. Jesus is never patient with the conventional wisdom of religious practice and leadership.

The foregoing illustration is a long way around to arrive at the conclusion that incarnational, or relational, ministry has little to do with how one frames or packages the message. As Marshall McLuhan said, "The medium *is* the message," but here the medium is the person as well as the situation, or context. What does this irreducible datum of the Christian witness genuinely signify for both the theory and practice of evangelism?

One of the current buzzwords in what might be loosely characterized as the buzz marketing of the new and improved postmodern church is the adjective *missional*. These days every Christian community that wants in some legitimate sense to be au courant is beginning to define itself with this very adjective. The expression clearly is a direct adaptation of the traditional and quite familiar ecclesiological word "mission," from which we derive "missionary." The tacit implication in the present popularity of the term is that churches must be much more than simply self-standing and self-serving organizations attentive mainly to the needs and desires of their attendees. They must incessantly reach out to those who are beyond the fringes of established Christianity, and they must do so in a way that is integral rather than incidental to their mission and purpose. After all, is that not what the Great Commission ultimately comes down to?

Is it not more than a little ironic, however, that churches in the postmodern—or post-Christendom—world should have to mold themselves as "missional" at all? In its historic sweep Christianity has always been missional. The command to make disciples, routinely confused in evangelical circles with planting churches, is seamlessly stitched with the command to love one's neighbor as oneself. Discipling shows what God's love in the person of Jesus, who is the Christ, is really all about. That is the true *missio Dei*. According to Darrell Guder, "The missional church works in the world to show God's love and compassion to others outside the church. God's love is too great to be kept only within the church; it has to be shared."[17]

Sharing Christ's Love, or Becoming as Christs

But how one actually shares Christ's love is what is really at stake. The dilemma harks back to Jesus's own ministry, when he was confronted with the pragmatic question of how one actually shows authentic love of neighbor, the impetus of the Great Commandment. Jesus answers as he often does, in completely astonishing fashion, with an illustration, this time concerning the Good Samaritan. As with so many of the repetitions of the commandment in Jesus's teaching ministry, the anecdote thoroughly radicalizes what has probably become a somewhat blasé rendering of the Great Commandment. Our response could never prove as stunning or as outré as Jesus's own story, but it will probably still be shocking to the average Christian who muses over the true ramifications. For the church to share God's love according to a missional model may mean to let go of and do away with all the familiar and formal trappings of Christian, or church-related and church-driven, programs, projects, and activities and to let the medium (the person of Christ Jesus) be thoroughly the message.

The model for a truly missional, or incarnational, community can be found in Paul's exhortation to the church at Colossae. Contemporary writers who are seeking to elaborate such a model cite Paul's Epistle to the Colossians. Paul begins by commending the Colossians for "the love you bear towards all God's people" (Col. 1:4 NEB). As anyone who has carefully studied this relatively brief epistle knows, Paul attributes the success of such a missional community to a "secret" (*mystērion*). The ancient mysteries were tightly guarded rituals and initiations that frequently involved face-to-face encounters in underground chambers with an invisible divine presence. Paul regularly uses the term, particularly in Colossians and

17. Darrell L. Guder, ed., *Missional Church: A Vision for the Sending of the Church in North America* (Grand Rapids: Eerdmans, 1998), 135.

Ephesians, to describe the relationship between Christ and the people
of God.

In Colossians the secret, or mystery, is the incarnation itself, which
achieves its fullness not just in the life, death, and resurrection of
Jesus but also in the church itself.

> He is the image of the invisible God; his is the primacy over all
> created things. In him everything in heaven and on earth was cre-
> ated, not only things visible but also the invisible orders of thrones,
> sovereignties, authorities, and powers; the whole universe has been
> created through him and for him. And he exists before everything,
> and all things are held together in him. He is, moreover, the head
> of the body, the church. He is its origin, the first to return from the
> dead, to be in all things alone supreme. For in him the complete
> being of God, by God's own choice, came to dwell. Through him
> God chose to reconcile the whole universe to himself, making peace
> through the shedding of his blood upon the cross—to reconcile all
> things, whether on earth or in heaven, through him alone. (Col.
> 1:15–20 NEB)[18]

But the *mystērion* is not simply cosmic; it is also interpersonal.
Paul goes on to say that his role as the apostle to the gentiles has
been all along to deliver the "message" (*logos*) of the richness of
the person of Jesus "in full" (*plērōsai*). As messenger, Paul makes
manifest "the secret hidden for long ages and through many generations, but now disclosed to God's people, to whom it was his will
to make it known—to make it known how rich and glorious it is
among all nations. The secret is this: *Christ in you*, the hope of a
glory to come" (Col. 1:25–27 NEB, emphasis added). In short, the
mystery of the incarnation is constantly unfurling in the body of
believers who affirm the message of the gospel, which is not a verbal
content so much as it is the embodiment of love in active relationship, of "being Jesus" to others. Becoming a missional community
has little to do with church outreach beyond one's neighborhood,
or national borders. It has everything to do with shattering walls
and barriers between people, even the barriers put up by the often-
fulsome chatter of evangelism.

18. For a postmodern reading of Colossians along these lines, see Brian Walsh and
Sylvia Keesmaat, *Colossians Remixed: Subverting the Empire* (Downers Grove, IL:
InterVarsity, 2004).

Incarnational ministry in a globopomo setting, therefore, means setting aside even the Christian/non-Christian distinction, particularly when being a Christian turns out to be a barrier against being Christ to one another. As we are "constantly renewed in the image of [our] Creator and brought to know God," there can be "no question . . . of Greek and Jew, circumcised and uncircumcised, barbarian, Scythian, slave and freeman," inasmuch as "Christ is all, and is in all" (*panta kai en pasin*; Col. 3:10–11 NEB). To be a Christ-follower and a discipler implies that we are manifesting Christ's fullness in a fully relational sense in all our thoughts and deeds. At the conclusion of the treatise *The Freedom of a Christian*, the little book that became the manifesto of the Protestant Reformation of the sixteenth century, Martin Luther espoused the radical meaning of incarnational Christianity when he declared that as Christians we must be "Christs to each other." We are to each other, and the other is to us, what Luther calls a *larva*, a "mask" of the holy. Luther's insight anticipates by four centuries the postmodern philosopher Emmanuel Lévinas's notion that the face of the Other is the portal to the holy. As Christ, who was God, became one of us, so his infinite love flows through us in our self-giving relation to the Other. In Luther's words, "As our heavenly Father has in Christ freely come to our aid, we also ought freely to help our neighbor through our body and its works, and each one should become as it were a Christ to the other that we may be *Christs to one another* and Christ may be the same in all, that is, that we may be truly Christians."[19]

To be a Christian is not simply to believe in the divinity of Jesus or to subscribe to a certain set of doctrines, although historically these epistemic tests of the faith have not been inconsequential. It is both to reveal Christ in who we are and to see the face of Christ in those we encounter. That is incarnational Christianity in the lived, not just the dogmatic, sense. It is what we ultimately mean by the GloboChrist, the Christ that is in us, and through us, and with us, and for us, the God who is simultaneously in immanent and transcendent relation with us.

Indeed, the incarnation is the secret of how the whole of historic Christianity has spread and developed in a dazzling diversity of cultures and how it continues to spread and develop throughout the

19. *Luther's Works*, ed. Jaroslav Pelikan (Philadelphia: Muhlenberg Press, 1957), 31:367–68, emphasis added.

world, according to former missionary Andrew Walls. He argues that the very doctrine of the incarnation entails a constant "translation" of who God is into seemingly disparate and incompatible cultures. Christianity has no culture itself but belongs to all cultures. "Incarnation is translation. When God in Christ becomes man, divinity was translated into humanity, as though humanity were a receptor language."[20]

He continues: "Translation involves the attempt to express the meaning of the source from the resources of, and within the working system of, the receptor language. Something new is brought into the language, but that new element can only be comprehended by means of and in terms of the pre-existing language and its conventions. In the process that language and its system is effectively expanded, put to new use; but the translated element from the source language has also, in a sense, been expanded by translation." Following the linguistic comparison, we add that "Christ was not simply a loanword adopted into the vocabulary of humanity; he was fully translated, taken into the functional system of the language, into the fullest reaches of personality, experience, and social relationship."[21]

The comparison is more than incidental because it points to what might ultimately be involved in taking an incarnational approach to fulfilling the Great Commission. If relationality in the deep sense that Jesus intended is both medium and message, then we cannot formulate the translation project in terms of any sort of theology or theological hermeneutics but only in terms of how Christ is expressed in myriad cultural contexts. Many Western pastors and professionals have the mistaken impression that a proper theology of culture would somehow facilitate such a project. But we are not concerned with any theological *logos* here. It is a matter of the Logos "becoming flesh" in the most profound understanding of the phrase.

The Semiotic Project

Westerners may have such a difficult time comprehending the new wave of Christianity in developing countries because they presume

20. Andrew F. Walls, *The Missionary Movement in Christian History* (Maryknoll, NY: Orbis Books, 1996), 27.
21. Ibid., 28.

that the translation project can only be carried through in their own grammar and syntax. Western theology has historically been joined at the hip with Greek philosophy, which in turn is built on the Indo-European language structure, with its subject-predicate sentence construction, inferential logic, and conceptual classification system. In the 1960s certain younger and now quite well-known philosophers in Germany and France, influenced by the latest cultural anthropology and sophisticated studies in comparative linguistics, began to recognize that the habitual prototype of philosophical reasoning and argument was insufficient to account for the vertiginous pace of intellectual change and social transformation then under way in the West. Their innovative and often highly idiosyncratic modes of doing philosophy, not to mention theology, came to be known as "postmodernist" in both substance and style. The postmodernists themselves eventually came to disparage the old school as "modernism," regarded as an excessively formal and overly generalized methodology. Western philosophy and theology up to that time seemed largely to be imprisoned within the modernist model.

In his famous essay "White Mythology," Jacques Derrida put it this way:

> Metaphysics—the white mythology which reassembles and reflects the culture of the West: the white man takes his own mythology, Indo-European mythology, his own *logos*, that is, the *mythos* of his idiom, for the universal form of that he must still wish to call Reason. Which does not go uncontested. . . . White mythology—metaphysics has erased within itself the fabulous scene that has produced it, the scene that nevertheless remains active and stirring, inscribed in white ink, an invisible design covered over in the palimpsest.[22]

The aim of the "White Mythology" essay was to break through the anvil grip of Western philosophy as a form of "logicism" and to show that human language is far richer and does far more than the heirs of Aristotle, with their focus on propositions and the categories used in rational system-building, could envision. As was common in that period, Derrida dwelt on the distinctive properties of rhetorical and metaphorical speech, which he contrasted with deductive demonstration. Metaphor is based, Derrida writes, not on the relation-

22. Jacques Derrida, *Margins of Philosophy*, trans. Alan Bass (Chicago: University of Chicago Press, 1982), 213.

ship between the universal and the particular, the general and the
specific, or the word and the thing to which it refers, as is the case
in Western philosophical analysis, but on "the resemblance between
two signs, one of which designates the other."[23] This investigation of
the contextual and functional relationship between two signs is what
has come in contemporary philosophical literature to be known as
"semiotics." The bulk of what we now call postmodern philosophy
mirrors this fault-line shift from propositional logic to semiotics.

But what does this semiotic turn in philosophy—and by extension
in theology—have to do with the broader topic we are considering—
the postmodern turn in ministry and mission? It has everything to
do with it. In their introduction to a provocative set of essays on
the new Pentecostalism around the globe, André Corten and Ruth
Marshall-Fratani explain that the new world Christianity can be
appraised only as a facet of globalization overall. Globalization
itself is a vast and sweeping ocean current that compels an entirely
new form of theoretical discourse suitable to the multifaceted phenomena it embraces.

> Globalisation opens up new worlds as processes of migration and
> mass mediation accompany new forms of wealth and accumulation,
> opening wide vistas of possible lives, inciting desire and fantasy, but
> also anxiety, frustration, downward mobility and insecurity. . . . The
> force of contemporary Pentecostalism and the reason for its remark-
> able growth seems to lie partly in this capacity to embody the open-
> endedness of a global network of flows, a composite of heterogeneous
> elements flexible and indeterminate enough in meaning to allow their
> setting to work in a multitude of contexts, yet offering at the same
> time a stable collection of narrative formulae and well-organized
> structures which provide a solid anchorage for individuals at large
> in the frightening sea of possibilities and frustrations.[24]

The phraseology of "global network of flows" is reminiscent of
Deleuze, who recognized that meaning and signification in a real, historical sense have virtually nothing to do with the subject-predicate,
subject-object, or speech-referent relationship of both classical and

23. Ibid., 215.
24. André Corten and Ruth Marshall-Fratani, eds., *Between Babel and Pentecost: Transnational Pentecostalism in Africa and Latin America* (Bloomington: Indiana University Press, 2001), 3.

modern Western philosophy. Such a philosophy is our own "white mythology," which remains inadequate—regardless of how much we strain to theologize—to the next postmodern Christendom, which is moving south while substantially altering the demographics of faith throughout the planet. Signs are not anchored in concepts; they are fluid and changeable. As the nineteenth-century philosopher Friedrich Nietzsche, who laid the ground plan for postmodernism, put it so aptly, language is not a fortress of reason but a "mobile army of metaphors."

Semiotics instructs us how to read the signs of the times, or more precisely, the de-signs of the times. Deleuze's notion of rhizomic patterns of growth underscores both the mobility and metaphoricity of all human expression. The establishment of the Internet as the framework for all contemporary communications yields the explosion across all formerly isolated *ethnē*, territories, and terrains as a global network culture. This culture, in turn, has its own language—the language of political icons, advertising images, electronic media clips—subject to a semiotic reading. Culture can be read semiotically. And the presence of Christ can be both read and deciphered within those cultures. The indigenization of global Christianity requires such a deciphering. Often what comes across as Christian by this undertaking seems to us not to be Christian at all if we invoke traditional liturgical, theological, or ecclesiastic criteria, much of which derives from an original indigenization of the faith first in Mediterranean and later in European societies.

Our doubts, however, are more theological than evangelical. In today's new African Christianity, it is not unprecedented for both leaders and recent converts to pray to ancestors, an old and ubiquitous practice, at the same time as they recite the Lord's Prayer or invoke the name of Christ. In the early 1990s I had a striking experience of this sort among American Indians when I attended an enormous, national conference in Albuquerque, New Mexico, of teachers and educational administrators representing a broad spectrum of the major tribes. At the start of a sumptuous banquet for all the conference attendees, the presiding Indian dignitary said a blessing for the meal, and he concluded the prayer with the words "in the name of Jesus, the Great Spirit who has watched over our peoples since the dawn of creation."

Scholars would dub this kind of prayer as an example of "religious syncretism." We can define syncretism as the fusion of

distinctly different and often incompatible types of religious belief
or conduct. In the Western scholarly and theological perspective,
syncretism is usually dismissed as something that cheapens authentic Christianity, even though church history from the writings
of Paul all the way down to present-day televangelism has been
dependent on the syncretic combination and adaptation of disparate values, practices, and attitudes. However, the prevalence of
indigenized forms of faith throughout history makes one wonder
what exactly is the authentic kernel of Christianity that syncretism
somehow degrades.

In its very heart and soul, Christianity is syncretistic to the
extent that the royal ideal of the Jewish Messiah was at the out-
set combined with the familiar Hellenistic motif of the dying
and rising god, which was much more congenial to the tastes of
the earliest gentile Christians than the barely intelligible idea of
an imperial savior for the Jewish nation. As Jenkins observes,
even ancestor worship, which some commentators have identified as essential to the "primal spirituality" underlying the new
global Christianity, can be taken in this fashion. "For the African
churches, the notion of continuity with the world of the ancestors is not only credible, it is a fundamental component of the
belief system." In addition, "that believers regularly see their
dead ancestors in dreams and visions is taken as proof that the
deceased are still alive in God. Closeness to native traditions gives
a powerful relevance to the corporate and communal visions of
the church, the *ecclesia*."[25]

Scripture says little about the need to preserve an "authentic Christianity," although the New Testament does constantly
warn about the perils of false prophets and false teachers. What
it consistently emphasizes is that all must, and in the end will,
call on the name of Jesus—and Jesus alone—as their Savior. The
name of Jesus cannot be substituted for Allah, or Amitabah, or
Vishnu. Jesus is "King of kings and Lord of lords." In other words,
the name of Jesus is the semiotic connecting point for all other
genres of religious endeavor, which come to assume a radically
new texture of meaning when woven together with the narrative
of Christ's ministry, crucifixion, resurrection, and ascent to the
heavenlies.

25. Jenkins, *The Next Christendom*, 133.

What Is Semiotics?

Before we advance any further with this theme, it would probably be helpful to explore what exactly semiotics is and has been as a minor branch of philosophy that has telling implications for postmodern theological thinking. The study of signs is as old as Western thought itself and has its roots in Platonism. It is first elaborated with a certain sophistication in Christian theology by Augustine of Hippo, who was the first major thinker to sketch the principles of what today we would call biblical hermeneutics, or interpretation. Augustine was concerned that the Bible, now both available and familiar to all citizens of the post-Constantinian Empire, would be misconstrued by those still under the spell of paganism.

Augustine was worried that many would "know" the biblical texts without understanding them and thereby take everything literally and become confused or plunge into doctrinal error. "Having become familiar with the language of Divine Scriptures, we should turn to those obscure things which must be opened up and explained so that we may take examples from those things that are manifest to illuminate those things which are obscure."[26] In the founding epoch of world Christianity, Augustine realized that divine revelation is never simply commensurate with the dictates of common sense, an insight grossly neglected by today's evangelical inerrantists and fundamentalists. And the way to bridge this gap is through an approach that we would now identify as a crude instance of semiotics. "There are two reasons why things written are not understood: they are obscured either by unknown or by ambiguous signs."[27]

According to Augustine, a comparison of the order of signs (some obscure and others not so obscure) is the solution to the interpretation of texts. Augustine's recommendations, loosely speaking, were heeded with different degrees of enthusiasm and novelty by later medieval and Scholastic theologians and ultimately led to relatively advanced theories of language that flowered in such later philosophical and theological movements as Thomism, nominalism, Protestantism, empiricism, and pragmatism. Some of these move-

26. Augustine of Hippo, *On Christian Doctrine*, trans. D. W. Robertson Jr. (Indianapolis: Bobbs-Merill, 1958), 2.9.42.
27. Ibid., 2.10.43.

ments, by the same token, can be considered the direct ancestors of postmodernism.

Charles Sanders Peirce, an American philosopher who never produced any systematic body of writings, gave the word *semiotics* wide currency and defined it as something with broader implications than what it had previously connoted in the history of thought. Peirce saw the theory of signs as essential to exploring the nature and mechanisms of human communication, not just thought and language in the abstract. Under the influence of the twentieth-century French researcher Ferdinand de Saussure, semiotics evolved as a means to investigate forms of communication that are not bound up with the grammar and syntax of human languages, even though Saussure himself was a linguist. One more esoteric version of the field in recent years has been *biosemiotics*, which examines communication at the level of subhuman organisms. In the social sciences and humanities, semiotics has served to promote the study of culture without the classic biases of the separate disciplines. Semiotics is capable of making sense out of how people meaningfully experience everything from painting and cinema to television advertising and haute cuisine without making cumbersome philosophical assumptions.

One of the factors behind the flourishing of semiotics was Saussure's dictate that signs are not the same as simple descriptors. Even Peirce presumed, as had philosophers before him, that signs have some material relationship to that which they signify, as smoke does to fire. But Saussure insisted that signs are arbitrary: they are bare conventions. Saussure did not push this precept to argue for a doctrine of philosophical, moral, or cultural relativism. His point was that signs and things belong to different strata of reality, which these days is intuitively obvious, now that through advances in linguistic science we can appreciate the intricacies of the various human languages and the porous boundary between verbal and nonverbal communication. It was a point that Augustine also grasped when he came up against the disparity between natural reason and the mysteries of God's revelation.

The greatest mystery—or *mystērion*, in Paul's argot—for the Christian faithful is the divine incarnation in Christ. The role of semiotics in both the practice of incarnational ministry and a postmodern global incarnational theological mind-set, which is both evangelical and "catholic" in the original creedal sense of the term, is beginning to loom in sight. The warrant arises out of the Great

Commission itself. Making disciples of all nations entails "dwelling" or "tabernacling"—the language used over and over in the Johannine literature—with others in their unique situation, in their culture, their language, their dress, their perceptual habits, just as God "was in Christ" and dwelt, and continues to dwell, and will always dwell with us as Emmanuel, as God with us. We can dwell—and dwelling requires the kind of radical relationality that Jesus demonstrates to us—only when we understand God's "de-sign" for our lives and his de-signs that encompass our cultural and communicative connections with others. Semiotics is not an obscure kind of academic undertaking, as admittedly it has often been. It is more than a blueprint for practical or pastoral ministry. It is the cipher for indigenizing our faith wherever the opportunity may present itself.

3

Utter Holiness
or Wholly Otherness

Finding Fidelity among the Infidels

> Each culture has its ultimate, and Christ is the
> ultimate in everyone's vocabulary.
>
> Andrew Walls

Indigenizing the Gospel

The problem with being missional is that sharing the gospel
in a postmodern world requires that the Christian confront the
overwhelming plurality of non-Christian faiths or anti-Christian
prejudices. The old colonial idea of evangelism was to find a captive
audience of the unsaved among native populations, then persuade
them that they were languishing in darkness and in error and that
only the "Christian"—usually meaning white, European—way of
thinking would lead them to the light.[1] The postcolonial situation
has been frequently the reverse. When decolonization commenced

1. The persistence of this approach made major national news in 1999 when the
International Mission Board of the Southern Baptist Convention came out with "prayer
guides" to non-Christian religions that made the following statements, for example,

after the Second World War and reached its crest during the three decades that followed, Christianity among the developing nations underwent a process of "indigenization" that ultimately disestablished it from colonial administration, organization, and practice while sparking momentum and growth that it had never authentically experienced in the past.

But indigenization has also meant assimilation of what were hitherto considered heathen icons, values, and cultural practices. The same thing happened when Catholic Christianity burgeoned during the Constantinian era among the peasantry and ultimately spread into Northern Europe and the Americas. As we have argued, patristic Christianity itself represented an indigenization—or hellenization—of the original gospel proclamation. Meanwhile, from the turn of the twentieth century onward, Christianity has been in retreat throughout the old colonial citadels of Europe—and to a lesser extent in the United States—before the cannonade of secularism and has been penetrated by new, consumer-styled and media-packaged forms of indigenous, non-Christian religiosity, or what have in the past been called "new religions," "alternative altars," or even "cults."

How does a postmodern Christian propagate the message in this teeming bazaar of spiritual options, intimations, and lifestyles? How does one fulfill the Great Commission in the midst of cultural fission and fragmentation? How is it possible to remain Christlike in carrying the gospel to all nations when Western Christendom as we know it is no more and its idols have been thoroughly deconstructed by global, consumer culture. What might a reenergized postmodern Jesus movement look like when there is progressively less difference not just between Athens and Jerusalem but also between Hollywood and Bollywood, when in South Asian culture Christ can barely be distinguished from Krishna, when the quest for utter holiness in a media-saturated world is confounded by the wholly otherness of other religions and diverse religious cultures?

So we ask, WWPD—what would Paul do? Or WWPPDD—what would a postmodern Paul dare to do?

Much of the discussion over this issue has been blissfully avoided among Christian writers, chiefly because the standard theological

---

about Hinduism: "Hindus lack a concept of sin or personal responsibility." There is a "darkness in their Hindu hearts that no lamp can dispel."

view has been that only a pure Christian proclamation—and the standards of purity are often spun out by modern theological considerations—can both compete with and be expected to push back the idolatries of other faiths, or faith-languages. Such a view conforms in principle, if not necessarily in practice, to the thrust of the Christian evangel of the early centuries. The Christian evangelist is remarkably in a situation comparable to what Paul was up against during the first century. There is no longer any Christendom that might serve as a base for evangelical expansion into the "darker" regions of the planet. Indeed, regions such as Africa, which came to be known as the "dark continent" during the heyday of European colonial domination and militant endeavors to convert what Western missionaries considered to be "backward" peoples, is now where the light of the gospel is shining the brightest. After the collapse of Communism in 1991, a sanguine outlook prevailed throughout the West that global capitalism—which no longer resembled what Marxists had clamored to bring crashing down—and the gestation of international markets for goods, services, and capital flows would be the pervasive force to spur rapid globalization. Marxist societies from China to Vietnam to the former Eastern European bloc marketized themselves overnight, and competitive and entrepreneurial energies were unleashed. Soviet-style command economies vanished from the scene, to be supplanted by volatile and frequently corrupt industrial and financial oligarchies, many of which were simply new ways of dressing up privileged and powerful Communist elites, who carried on with what critics dubbed "crony capitalism."

Globalization was prophesied by the new-worldly philosophers of the 1990s as an unstoppable juggernaut of the liberal Western economic model. During this period the explosion of the global economy seemed adequate testament to this trend. Political scientist Benjamin Barber sarcastically branded this development the coming of "McWorld." At least in the West, McWorld involves the replacement of democratic civil societies by transnational corporations that advance their octopus-like reach by manipulating private consumer preferences, desires, and fantasies. Barber contrasted the emergence of McWorld with what he labeled "jihad," referring not to the phenomenon of militant Islamism that has crowded our attention since 2001, but to tribalism, religious and ethnic conflict, and the revival of ancient hatreds and particularized grievances of the kind encountered during the Yugoslavian civil wars of that decade.[2]

But as we are now seeing, globalization is not necessarily equivalent to Westernization. In fact, as the surge in Islamist sentiment and the leftward political tilting of Latin America indicates, globalization is intimately bound up in some quarters with anti-Westernization. Very little of the new anti-Western sentiment has anything to do with nationalism, which seems to be definitely on the wane worldwide. It is really the counterpunch of the developing world to the economic conditions of rapid development, particularly the depredations suffered by the world's impoverished masses. This counterpunch has been struck not so much by political or economic means and rhetoric as through religion.

Returning to Paul, we can conclude that the world today is analogous in a number of important ways to the Roman imperium of the first century. At the time of Caesar Augustus, who for the most part initiated the pax Romana, the limits of empire had been attained, although few Hellenists could foresee that eventuality, and the surrounding civilization as a whole had acquiesced to such a state of affairs. As one adage goes, the fruits of success end up scattering the seeds of destruction. It was certainly the case with Rome. Roman cultural and political hegemony engendered fierce resentment and finally revolt, first among the Jews and then among the northern barbarians on the other side of the *limina*, the official boundary stones of civilization. Largely the same forces also propelled the rapid diffusion of Christianity first among the underclasses and subsequently among the clerical bureaucracy of the empire. This revolt was not an armed insurgency, as in the case of the Jewish wars. It was a moral and spiritual revolt in the name of a deity the Romans could only hate because Jesus the Nazarene was so unlike anything they had ever encountered, and because he motivated his devotees to be glorified through suffering, martyrdom, and a determination that their overseers could scarcely comprehend.

As historians of Christianity have reminded us for generations, from Palestine to the Baltic the new faith expanded into a permanent vacuum fostered by a general social uneasiness concerning

2. See Benjamin Barber, *Jihad versus McWorld: How Globalism and Tribalism Are Reshaping the World* (New York: Ballantine Books, 1996).

the breakdown of tribal and ethnic identities that the pax Romana
had created. Technological, political, and economic strategies can
attack chronic poverty when cultural systems remain intact, but at
times of deep popular stress resulting from cultural dissolution,
only faith is capable of stepping into the breach. What we are now
realizing is that the measurable economic improvements in people's
lives, or at least improvements in economic opportunities spurred
by the fall of Communism and the new momentum that event gave
to global capitalism, was ultimately overshadowed by the deficits
attaching to the cultural dislocations that globalization has brought
in its wake.

The biggest challenge and opportunity for Paul's mission to the
gentiles was cultural disenfranchisement. Many of the first Christians were diaspora Jews far removed from Palestine, who regarded
themselves still as Jews, but as Jews who had always smarted from
the disdain felt from their brothers in Judea who controlled the central temple. According to historians, they were the first converts in
Paul's mission to the gentiles. Christianity aided them in overcoming
this cultural identity crisis. After the destruction of the temple, the
door was definitely opened for non-Jews to assume a Jewish identity, which had been denied to them by the Jews themselves, who
looked down on the *gôyîm*. Judaism, with its radical monotheistic
bent, its solid "family values," and its relative economic prosperity,
had always been a source of envy and emulation among pagans.[3]
Paul's genius was always expressed through his ability to preach a
universal gospel that could be credibly customized—we would say
indigenized—among particular worldviews, all the while retaining
its Jewish marrow.

In short, Christianity flourished because it was able to absorb—
through the Christ principle enunciated in Colossians and through
the kind of incarnational ministry we have already commended—
rather than expel many elements from the rainbow continuum of
world religions that predominated at the time. The staggering nature
of this feat has often gone unappreciated by Christian scholarship
of all stripes, principally because the early centuries of the faith have
usually been dissected through Protestant eyes.

3. See Rodney Stark, *The Rise of Christianity: How the Obscure, Marginal Jesus
Movement Became the Dominant Religious Force* (San Francisco: HarperSanFrancisco,
1997).

The Protestant Reformation represented a search within the context of late medieval thinking to recover an original or apostolic Christianity shorn of all the worldly and Roman features that the church had allegedly acquired since the conversion of Constantine. Protestant researchers, especially in Germany throughout the nineteenth and early twentieth centuries, pioneered the now familiar historical-critical method of modern-day biblical scholarship that precipitated a "battle for the Bible" in America before and after World War I, dividing the house between modernists and fundamentalists—as they were called at the time—or liberals and evangelicals, the present preferred nomenclature. They also forged the field of inquiry that came to be known as the history of religions, which supposedly examined all the world religious traditions from a neutral perspective and did not seek, at least overtly, to impose the prejudices of Christian theology upon them.

But the bias of Protestant thought remained. According to historian of religion Jonathan Z. Smith, this bias has warped the lens by which we look at early Christianity. Evangelical thought, which has had little truck with the history of religions except perhaps for apologetic purposes, has in a quite different fashion amplified this bias. Smith maintains that early Christianity, particularly the writings of Paul, cannot be separated so easily from the matrix of Mediterranean religious practice, as scholars have been apt to do. Researchers have habitually endeavored to invoke a principle of comparison, making a rigid distinction between the gospel and the mystery religions that were everywhere around Paul and the earliest Christian congregations. "We can formulate the principle of comparison that has informed the majority of scholarship in this area as follows: 'apostolic Christianity' and 'Protestantism' are 'unique'; the religions of Late Antiquity, most especially the 'mysteries' and 'Catholicism,' are the 'same.'"[4]

In short, the mysteries are something alien to the pure evangel that Jesus preached and Paul promoted along with the other apostles and evangelists. But this distinction is a relic of the Protestant theological agenda, we might infer from Smith's very detailed and extensively documented analysis, and does not accurately reflect the history of early Christianity itself. Because the work of these scholars was

4. Jonathan Z. Smith, *Drudgery Divine: On the Comparison of Early Christianities and the Religions of Late Antiquity* (Chicago: University of Chicago Press, 1990), 45.

embedded in an ongoing anti-Catholic polemic centering on the Roman church's presumed co-opting of the Bible by a focus on priestly ceremonies and sacraments, they failed to realize that the early church betokened what we would call the first real instance of an indigenized Jesus.

Paul uses the word *mystērion* repeatedly in his letters to characterize what Luther would later term the *sanctorum communio*, the "communion of saints," what Protestants would designate as the "church invisible." The mysteries, or mystery religions, outside of Christianity were prestigious communities and rites, which were diverse and widespread and reworked the means of worshiping a very ancient or foreign deity in a novel and highly secretive manner. Devotees and initiates of the mysteries were forbidden, sometimes on pain of death, to divulge the content of these secret rites. The experience of induction and initiation often entailed the fostering of altered states of consciousness, though not necessarily by artificial or chemical means.

Christianity and the Mystery Religions

Once initiated into the mysteries, a follower would receive both a new esoteric identity and a powerful sense of belonging to a brotherhood or sisterhood. Modern college fraternities and sororities with their Greek letter names and hazing practices are holdovers from the ancient mysteries. So are adult fraternal orders such as the Masons. Leading examples of the mysteries observed during the age of empire were the cults of Isis, Osiris, Orpheus, Dionysus, and Mithra. The Eleusinian mysteries, which comprised a portion of Greece's religious establishment for centuries, had perhaps the largest population of practitioners. The Manichaeans were quite influential in the Eastern Empire during the third and later centuries AD, and the Gnostics—who flourished during the second century and later and upheld a doctrine of privileged, secret, and illumined knowledge (or *gnōsis*)—posed a formidable challenge to the growing Christian movement. The account of the mysteries given in the *Encyclopedia Britannica* stresses that they took origin in "tribal ceremonies" that were "performed by primitive peoples in many parts of the world." Their main purpose was to provide "common experiences" with the effect of a powerful sense of group solidarity.[5]

Scholars have tended to construe the emergence of Christianity and the evolution of the mystery cults as independent though parallel phenomena. While archaeology in recent years has gradually brought to light the concrete texture of religious life around the Mediterranean, investigators nonetheless have been able to make more educated guesses concerning what the mysteries might have actually looked like. Because of their clandestine character, the only real data available in the past had been what the church fathers, who were extremely critical, said about them. And observations of how Christianity is taking root nowadays in what were once pagan, tribal cultures supplies some good fodder for speculating on how the process unfolded between AD 100 and 300. If Protestant prejudice has blinded Christian historians to the integral relationship between the mysteries and the transformation of what was at first an essentially Jewish type of piety, the indigenization of the faith in the developing world demands that we reassess the old notions.

The bald assertion that biblical faith language has always been intertwined with the mysteries was made over a half century ago by a young seminary student named Martin Luther King Jr. At this point we can only conjecture, but it is entirely possible that this "discovery," which has been preserved among King's papers and is either unknown or taken as having little importance among his admirers and biographers, had more to do than we realize with his successful transmutation of African Baptist Protestantism into an earthshaking crusade for social justice. As Philip Jenkins makes clear, the European—and American secular liberal—preference for private religious expression over any alliance between faith and politics has never had any resonance in the developing world, or the South, to use his terminology. That is because "during the twentieth century" it was always the case that "Third World churches came to be identified with the cause of reform or, frequently, revolution."[6]

At first indigenous Christianity sprouted the banners of anticolonialism, but in the postcolonial era we have seen it as adopt-

5. "Mystery Religion," *Encyclopædia Britannica* (2006). Encyclopædia Britannica Premium Service, August 10, 2006, http://www.britannica.com/eb/article-9108747.

6. Philip Jenkins, *The Next Christendom: The Coming of Global Christianity* (New York: Oxford University Press, 2002), 143.

ing a potent and prophetic stance against corrupt oligarchies and the excesses of globalization. Was King merely an early American harbinger of this trend, especially if we consider the civil rights movement itself as a kind of domestic anticolonialism? Or did King also have a more trenchant insight into what historical Christianity actually was that continues to be evident in the expansion of what Jenkins dubs the "next Christendom"?

In a research paper, King wrote that "Christianity triumphed over these mystery religions after long conflict. This triumph may be attributed in part to the fact that Christianity took from its opponents their own weapons, and used them: the better elements of the mystery religions were transferred to the new religion." He concluded his paper—which he wrote for the course "Development of Christian Ideas" at Crozer Theological Seminary in Philadelphia in early 1950—with the following observation: "The greatest influence of the mystery religions on Christianity lies in a different direction from that of doctrine and ritual. It lies in the fact that the mystery religions paved the way for the presentation of Christianity to the world of that time. They prepared the people mentally and emotionally to understand the type of religion which Christianity represented. . . . Christianity was truly indebted to the mystery religions for this contribution, for they had done this part of the groundwork and thus opened the way for Christian missionary work."[7]

The incarnational absorption of the mysteries into early Christianity is duplicated in a similar incorporation of indigenous forms of sacrality into the new global Christianity that makes up the next Christendom. Christianity has become a universalizing force that deterritorializes all local cults throughout the developing world. The new GloboChristianity is not impelled by opposition to empire in the same way it was in the first three centuries. It is driven by the hunger for an eternal identity amid the flux and decomposition of old empires and old certainties.

Christianity's remarkable capacity for speaking truth to heterogeneous and alien cultures through the indigenization of the faith can be illustrated in the work of Kang San Tan, who has worked

7. Excerpt from Clayborne Carson, Ralph E. Luker, and Penny A. Russell, eds., *The Papers of Martin Luther King, Jr.*, vol. 1 (Berkeley: University of California Press, 1992); quoted online at the publisher's Web site, http://www.stanford.edu/group/King/publications/papers/vol1/500215-The_Influence_of_the_Mystery_Religions_on_Christianity.htm.

for OMF International as director for missions research in Malaysia and is currently head of mission studies at Redcliffe College in the United Kingdom. He and his wife, Loun Ling, are well-known speakers and writers when it comes to world missions. Tan has been interested in the manner in which interfaith conversations, specifically with Buddhism in Southeast Asia, can actually serve as vehicles of incarnational evangelism. In the midst of these conversations, he insists, "one is challenged to live out the authentic Christian life in the context of full religious pluralism." In other words, one can be a good Christian and take the worldviews of Buddhism seriously without becoming either a New Age eclectic or one who essentially compromises the essence of one's own faith. "God's sovereignty as expressed in his kingship provides the basis for a missionary encounter with Buddhists. God, who is already the Heavenly King, must become king in the hearts of people." The Christian God is a king who shows unexpected and often unfamiliar mercy to those who cannot draw near to him because of prior belief systems that stand in the way. "Christians who are the recipients of God's mercy and who are worshippers of the righteous and holy God, have an epistemic and ethical duty to engage in dialogue with Buddhist people, even if they are atheistic or agnostic."[8]

On the surface Buddhists seem to be the last species of believers to whom Christians can seriously talk. With the exception of its historical folk variations that classically have been known as the Mahayana tradition, or "great vehicle," prevalent in East Asia, Buddhism is indeed an atheistic philosophy more than a religion consisting of a devotion to a particular deity or figure. Buddhism regards worship, or the fixation of the mind, on any divine being as a form of compulsive intellectual attachment. The aim of Buddhist meditation and Buddhist dharma, or way of life, is release from all desires and mental compulsions, including seemingly spiritual ones. The end of existence, according to Buddhism, is not what Christians would call beatitude, in the sense of an eternal relationship as a creature with their Creator God. It is nirvana, which implies the cessation of all motives, wishes, and cravings. A metaphor for nirvana is the snuffing out of a candle, with its flame signifying the

8. Kang San Tan, "A Kingdom-Oriented Framework for Encountering Buddhist World Views," paper presented at Bible and Nations Conference, Regent University, 2003.

active mind. In the Mahayana legacy, nirvana is conflated with the somewhat challenging concept of *sunyata*, or the "emptiness" of all thought and consciousness.

Thus the doxological formulation of Paul in Philippians "that at the name of Jesus every knee should bow, in heaven and on earth and under the earth, and every tongue confess that Jesus Christ is Lord, to the glory of God the Father" (Phil. 2:10–11) would sound fairly crazy, at least prima facie, to a Buddhist. According to Tan, however, there is room here for mediation that could be considered incarnational. Tan does not seem to buy into the tired nostrum of interfaith proponents that representatives of different religions need merely to understand one another while finding some sort of common ground. That is mere syncretism. Buddhism is a worthy interlocutor for Christians—as the famous Catholic monk and theologian Thomas Merton discovered over a generation ago—because it recognizes the limitations of human language and the failure of words to capture the essence of what is holy and infinite. Buddhists are not simple heathens. They can be shown, perhaps not apologetically but intuitively, that the name of Jesus to which a Christian bows is more than a piece of nomenclature. It is the absoluteness or wholly otherness behind all those forms of God that Buddhists reject. It is the name above all names, meaning that it brings into the realm of perceptible reality what that reality cannot contain. Christ, as Paul writes in Colossians, "is the image of the invisible God, the firstborn over all creation. For by him all things were created: things in heaven and on earth, visible and invisible, whether thrones or powers or rulers or authorities; all things were created by him and for him" (Col. 1:15–16). That is something a Christian can demonstrate meaningfully to a Buddhist, not just by one's words but also by one's own incarnate life.

Christ for Secular Europe

If Christians can be incarnational, "as Christs" for Buddhists and other non-Christian religions, then they can be the same for atheists and so-called secular humanists. One of the most difficult mission fields has always been Western Europe, with its culture of secularism and socialist humanism. Whereas Europeans have indeed been staunchly resistant—and remain so—to high-octane evangelism, which they identify with crude and bumptious American-style fundamentalism, what is often construed as the spiritual emptiness of life in the secular welfare state is fostering openness to the Christian message that appears unprecedented. The proverbial godlessness of Europe also, as Jenkins in his study of the state of the faith in Europe suggests, may also be something of a misconception. Jenkins writes that

> not even the most optimistic observer could pretend that European Christianity is in a healthy state, whether in comparison with global South societies, or with that great transatlantic anomaly, the United States. But institutional weakness is not necessarily the same as total religious apathy, and among all the grim statistics, there are some surprising signs of life. European Christians, after all, have the longest experience of living in a secular environment, and some at least attempt quite successfully to evolve religious structures far removed from older assumptions of Christendom.[9]

One American evangelist who is trying to evolve such structures in this context is David Acton, a Florida-based missionary who works for the international missions board of the Southern Baptists. Acton has been involved with missions in Eastern Europe and currently runs Hope for Sevilla in southern Spain. He works primarily with young people up to twenty-five years of age, some of whom are students, some of whom are employed. Previously he served as pastor for Scala-Gemeinde in Magdeburg, Germany, which used to be part of Communist East Germany. Scala-Gemeinde is largely a house church with ministry and worship services at the Café Latté Da am Uniplatz. The name Scala-Gemeinde (Community) derives from the empty Scala Kino (movie theater) in Magdeburg, which the group renovated and where they started meeting in 2003. The Web site goes on to give a fuller explanation of the name: "The word 'Scala' is Latin and means 'rock' or 'steps.' In the movie business it stands for the stepped rows of seats in the cinema hall. Yet for us it has another meaning. We want to be a rock for God in our city, and our community ought to be 'the steps to heaven' through which many people find the way to Jesus." But these steps are through the formation and maintenance of community. "Folks need to belong

9. Philip Jenkins, *God's Continent: Christianity, Islam, and Europe's Religious Crisis* (New York: Oxford University Press, 2007), 54.

before they believe," Acton says. That is why they did not "plant" a church so much as they sought to anchor the presence of Christ in a place that represents the heart and soul of the "secular city." "The cinema is not supposed to be just a place of worship, but also a hub where people come together in community and in relationship, a place where one can meet one another and God. Our motto goes: *Kirche-Kino-Kultur-Kaffee* [church, cinema, culture, coffee]."[10]

But Scala-Gemeinde is not just about community, or *Gemein-schaft*, a German word that has profound and complex connotations not easily imported into English. *Gemeinschaft* means both "community" and "communion." It can also be translated as "fellowship." The idea of Scala-Gemeinde seems to point toward a genuine God-encounter through the fullness and richness of relationships. Although at one level this approach may strike the casual observer as some kind of social gospel with an evangelical emphasis and a postmodern twist, it is precisely the opposite. Acton points out that when he and his wife arrived in Magdeburg, they discovered that the region was a blank slate: seventy-two percent of the inhabitants were atheists, a carryover from all the years of Soviet Communism. There was no obvious resonance with standard Christian worship, even of the contemporary variety, or even negative attitudes about church services for that matter, since the "Ossies" (former East Germans) never had any experience with what we consider church. So the Actons decided to throw out the book when it came to ministry. They could not follow the familiar Willow Creek model of seeker-sensitive services aimed at people who might be more comfortable with some sort of worship-lite, inasmuch as entrants into their *Gemeinde* would have nary a clue as to what exactly was being watered down to begin with. Instead, they opted to make worship a show or an event that might somehow provoke curiosity and over time actual participation. The Actons termed this process "pre-discipleship," an "invitation to experience God." "You can't talk about spiritual things until you've experienced them," Acton says. He tells the story of a sixty-five-year-old former Communist military officer who had observed worship and was fascinated. "You should see what they do on Sunday morning," he began telling people. Real and authentic community was something the Ossies— who in past lives had always worried about informers and the secret

10. Quoted from the Web site http://www.scala-gemeinde.de/14.0.html.

police and now often felt displaced in the new consumerist society of a unified Germany—were hungering for. But this sense of community could not be solidified without the powerful experience of worship, which was something entirely new to them. "All of a sudden they have the aha experience," Acton reports. "That is the Holy Spirit working."

Another illustration of incarnational ministry in the European context is an ongoing project hosted by the Austrian Baptist Union. In July 2007 a delegation of young Austrian Baptists took a trip across Texas. Among various activities, they visited the Woodlawn Baptist Church in Austin, did some work at Mission Arlington, and took part in Super Summer—a leadership training experience for young people who show leadership promise—on the campus of Hardin-Simmons University in Abilene.

"I think the biggest effect is to show our Baptist family is much larger than this small minority in our country," said Dietrich Fischer-Dorl, head of the youth division of the Austrian Baptist Union. "Ministering is part of a Christian lifestyle.[11] The Union, which is part of the European Baptist Union, has 1,417 members, which amounts to a little more than twenty congregations in a nation of approximately eight million in which Roman Catholicism is the overwhelmingly dominant faith. Those congregations include six Romanian speaking congregations.

The Baptist movement, which started in the early seventeenth century in England, came to Germany in 1834 and to Austria in 1869. At first, for political reasons they were not known as "Baptists" but as *taufgesinnte Christen* ("Baptism-minded Christians"). For several decades after coming to Vienna the Baptists were routinely persecuted by the state authorities. House churches were raided and Bibles and other books were confiscated. There is no persecution today, but Austria still only recognizes "registered" religions. The Baptists are recognized, but they are commonly referred to as a cult by many traditional Austrians.

The Baptist movement ultimately stems from the writings and influence of Balthasar Hubmaier, who was the leading light of the Anabaptist movement as part of the Radical Reformation of the six-

11. John Hall, "Open Plains, Open Hearts Welcome Austrian Baptists to Texas," *The Baptist Standard* (August 17, 2007), http://www.baptiststandard.com/postnuke/ index.php?module=htmlpages&func=display&pid=6703.

teenth century. Hubmaier was burned at the stake in Vienna in 1528 for heresy. He was widely known for the motto which he inscribed on all his written works: *Die Wahrheit ist untödlich*, or "truth is immortal." Anabaptists challenged both the Catholic Church and such major Reformers as Luther, Calvin, and Zwingli on the matter of infant baptism. The term *Anabaptist* comes from the Greek word meaning "re-baptism." Anabaptists, like all of today's Baptists, believe that one cannot be baptized until properly understanding the significance of the practice after making a commitment to a personal relationship with Christ.

The Baptist Union of Austria has had a close association for years with the Baptist General Convention of Texas (which is different from the state Southern Baptist Convention) through the BGCT Texas Partnerships ministry. The trip might be considered a "ministry exchange." One of the main effects of the trip was to show how student ministry, and especially volunteer work among the poor, functions in the United States. And the Texas Baptists and other evangelical congregations in the state have been sending young people to Austria to learn how ministry and evangelism work in that country, where expectations, culture, and practices are significantly different. In many ways, more Americans need to go to Austria rather than the other way around if American Christians are to open themselves up to where the new globopomo world as a whole is headed.

Europe has a reputation among American evangelical churches as a tough place for missionaries, mainly because so much money has been spent trying to bring the people "to Christ" and, in their minds, there is so little to show for it. That, of course, may have as much to do with the attitudes and prejudices of American evangelicals as the outlook of Europeans in general, and Austrians in particular. The political, cultural, and financial leverage that a highly conservative Austrian Catholicism has over that country, which for almost a millennium was the center of the Holy Roman Empire, plays a considerable role. The long-term psychological impact of two world wars has also been a factor. But once-overconfident, if not sometimes arrogant, former American missionaries are discovering that relational or incarnational evangelism *does in fact work* in this setting. They had just never tried it before.

One young missionary from Texas who underwent his own unexpected "attitude adjustment" immediately after arriving in Austria in the autumn of 2007 is Cooper Taylor, a twenty-something who grew up in north suburban Dallas and attended Christian schools all his life, including Wheaton College in Illinois. Taylor now is connected closely to Fellowship of Joy in Arlington, Texas, an Assemblies of God congregation with a dynamic student ministry that has supported missionaries to Vienna outside of their denomination. "We fail to believe in a creative God," Taylor says, looking back on his own sort of "conversion" experience concerning missionary work after becoming frustrated, like most missionaries, at the beginning. "Instead of recognizing [the Austrians] have their own social and cultural networks, we say 'let's go save the natives.'" The latter results in digging one more missionary "grave." Successful ministry, Taylor asserts, "grows up out of time and relationships with people. We haven't had to be as sophisticated in the past, and as patient."[12]

Taylor lives and works in a large building that houses students from Vienna's world-famous music university next door and other college-age young people who are involved in *Projekt Gemeinde*, which literally means "Project [Christian] Community" or "Project Church" in the broader sense of the word implied in English. The house and *Projekt Gemeinde* are run by Walter and Andrea Klimt, who have been involved for years in student mission work. Walter is general secretary of the Austrian Union. Andrea, the senior pastor of *Projekt Gemeinde*, is a college lecturer who, along with a team from the church as well as secularized Catholics, has produced a truly revolutionary multicultural and interactive children's CD for learning about the Bible.

Projekt Gemeinde was first conceived as an extension of the primary student work given to the Klimts by House Bethel under the direction of the Baptist Union. House Bethel is the key to everything that takes place as part of *Projekt Gemeinde*. The house is a student dormitory, consisting not only of actively involved Christians from all around Austria and the world but also of those who, upon leaving home to study found themselves moving more and more to the fringes of an active life of faith. House Bethel is designed so that those students "moving toward the fringes" can have "a safe place to rediscover, for themselves, their place among the people of God," according to a statement from *Projekt Gemeinde*. "By design it is an environment which gives them room to discover and to think for themselves," that often was not afforded to them during their Christian upbringing.

12. Conversation with Cooper Taylor, December 15, 2007.

The project's inaugural move was to plant a church in the midst of these students for the purpose of undertaking social work and further evangelism. The first initiative, combining both emphases simultaneously, was to incorporate Afghan believers into the community, so that *Projekt Gemeinde* was not two different churches sharing one building but a single fellowship of brothers and sisters as believers in Christ. Although worship at *Projekt Gemeinde* is conducted in both Farsi and German, further efforts to integrate the two constituencies meld family services, combining Persian and German speakers, regular meal sharing, mixed cell groups, and church retreats of Persian and German speakers. *Sharing life* is the key term in all of these activities, says senior pastor Andrea Klimt. "We want all the richness of the multi-ethnic people of God in our local congregation."

Vienna, which houses the United Nations development agencies, is one of the key worldwide point-of-entry locations for asylum-seekers and for émigrés to Western Europe. It was breathtaking and amazing for me to participate in a service led by a group of Iranian and Afghan Christian refugees and hear sung in Farsi many of the popular and contemporary Christian songs with which today's emerging or postmodern churchgoers are familiar. The power of their praise and their enthusiasm for God was a sight that could not be easily forgotten.

Ministry in Austria that bears fruit demands listening to others and building relationships over time. It is absurd to talk about Austrians in general as "unsaved." Austria was one of the first "barbarian" regions in the late Roman period to turn to Christianity. It is not a matter of "knowing Christ." Christianity and Christian institutions have been around for over fifteen hundred years. "It's not about the 'missions trip,'" Taylor argues. The building of ministry in this context is an "organic growth." One has to put aside everything one has learned in missionary training and ask, what is God doing here, and how I can be a part of what he's doing? American missionaries frequently "lack confidence that the Gospel can make its own way." Moreover, one cannot simply say "Jesus offers the solution" to whatever happens to be the problem. Often many missionaries prejudge and say, "I'm going to show you the Jesus you need," rather than the Jesus who will show you the way, starting from the situation the seeker is in. Cooper tells the story of a young man living in the house who had been raised Catholic in the conventional manner, but was transformed into a genuine "believer" over time. His life was not changed by coming to the altar or by high-powered apologetics. The young man was a brilliant student and skeptic of virtually everything religious. One day it dawned on him that the Christlike love and perseverance of his American "missionary" friends was due to something working on the inside of them that he had not himself yet experienced. One day he simply announced that he was an entirely new person. It is "a slow subversion" of routine habits and patterns of thought, Taylor notes. That is what postmodern ministry often adds up to.[13]

A similar testimony is given by Jason Valdez, who before traveling to Austria had been on a theological and perhaps a spiritual roller-coaster, starting with a powerful charismatic conversion experience and moving in the direction of standard conservative evangelicalism, according to his own statement, "for help in re-visioning the world in light of this new cosmos in which God was radically present and involved." He attended the ultraconservative Criswell College in downtown Dallas and became preoccupied with theological issues and familiar Baptist disputes such as Scriptural inerrancy and women in ministry. In Austria he found Baptists having many of the same discussions but with an entirely different attitude and approach. "I experienced a special breathing room spiritually and intellectually at *Projekt Gemeinde*," he writes. "While in the States, I never had any desire to leave the orthodoxy of Christian faith. The problem was it seemed that everywhere the demand was to hurry up and close the circle of dogma, declare your colors, and come out in favor of one or another of the many theological systems . . . and be as sure as everyone else that all other comers were sub-Christian or near apostates at best." He continues: "On coming to Vienna I saw God's love in action in special ways, and no one made theological hairsplitting the ground of life together. Although often quite convinced of their stance on many issues, no one was making demands to think certain ways before we could have fellowship in Jesus' name."[14]

Valdez recently was made an associate pastor at *Projekt Gemeinde*. Once in Austria he discovered quickly how irrelevant many of the theological concerns of American evangelicals can be. "These are not problems in the local context." For a while he was "at the end" of himself, he says, and "basically exhausted with trying to be a disciple of Jesus in the old way." He adds that when it comes to reaching out

13. Ibid.
14. E-mail from Jason Valdez, December 29, 2007.

for and as Christ, "you can't close the system and draw the boundaries." Reading Colossians and understanding what it means to be made in the "image of God" changed Valdez. Jesus is the perfect image, and it is our job as Christians—and especially as missionaries—to embody that image. Prior to that realization, Valdez had been trying to live a "life of holiness" that became an impossible standard, as it was for Paul, and a barrier to communicating God to those who did not have similar standards. "Jesus lived in perfect vision of his father," Valdez explains, "perfect understanding of what sin was. I shouldn't take that for granted. I don't find Jesus berating people who haven't accomplished that standard. Instead I find him rebuking those who draw the boundary line before it should be drawn. I watch Jesus, what he's doing. He is taking the burden of these people on himself." As a missionary "I make these other people my responsibility and I work for them before the throne of God."[15]

Valdez's passion for helping refugees and the marginalized grew out of his student work. Students are usually dismissed or patronized in the American church because they are considered resistant to formula gospel preaching and evangelism. But student work, according to Valdez, helps us understand the power and depth of how Christ works for and through people, how we can genuinely be Christs for each other. This insight was also formed after his coming to Austria from the reading of Dietrich Bonhoeffer, who along with Karl Barth has been the premier theological source of inspiration in Austria. "Bonhoeffer says God hates wish dreaming," Valdez quips. "God has an objective understanding of the church of Jesus Christ. Anyone who comes with his idea of church rather than what Jesus wants will become disillusioned with those people and with the God revolution that is happening here and in their understanding of what the people are in God's eyes."[16]

Rediscovering and honoring Christ in Europe's secular culture has been Pope Benedict's passion as well. It is something that Pope Benedict XVI, formerly Cardinal Joseph Ratzinger, has fervently stressed since he was elected pontiff in 2005. In his book *Europe: Today and Tomorrow*, Benedict warns of Europe's "imminent crisis of secularism" and asks, "Where do we go from here?" He stresses that militant secularism, both in its current libertarian and former Communist

15. Telephone conversation with Jason Valdez, December 17, 2007.
16. Ibid.

forms, has not led to personal liberation but to a self-destructive preoccupation with tolerance and cultural diversity, without any appreciation for the spiritual roots that make that attitude possible in the first
place. "We notice a self-hatred in the Western world that is strange
and that can be considered pathological." The West "no longer loves
itself; from now on it sees in its own history only what is blameworthy
and destructive, whereas it is no longer capable of perceiving what is
great and pure." He goes on: "Part of it is approaching with respect
the things that are sacred to others, but we can do this only if what
is sacred, God himself, is not foreign to us."[17]

If Europe cannot find its roots, if Christianity cannot re-indigenize
itself, even if only in the saeculum itself, the prospect is bleak. "For
the cultures of the world, the absolute secularity that has been taking shape in the West is profoundly foreign."[18] In Europe itself the
rekindling of Christianity has been stimulated, Jenkins among others
have emphasized, if only because of the challenge of Islam, which
is indigenizing in its own fashion among the sprawling immigrant
populations. The new GloboChristianity has an adversary as formidable as Caesar was in the first few centuries. Jenkins warns that
"the future centers of global population are chiefly in countries that
are already divided between the two great religions," Christianity
and Islam. "In present-day battles in Africa and Asia, we may today
be seeing the political outlines of the new century, and probably, the
roots of future great power alliances."[19] Jenkins talks ominously of
the possibility of a "war of the end of the world" between these two
religious "superpowers" in the developing South. The looming clash
is not just between the West and the rest, as Huntington believes,
but between the two historico-religious tectonic plates that comprise
Christian and Islamic visions of justice and the end times. The die
has been cast, and we ignore these forebodings at our own peril.
Thus before we explore any further what a global incarnational
Christianity might look like, we need to examine the depth of the
challenge it might be facing. We must address the challenge of what
has come to be called the postmodern Islamic revival. We must take
a peek through the so-called 10/40 Window.

17. Cardinal Joseph Ratzinger, *Europe: Today and Tomorrow* (San Francisco: Ig-
natius Press, 2004), 33.
18. Ibid., 34.
19. Jenkins, *The Next Christendom*, 164.

4

A Closer Look through the 10/40 Window

I think I came to see Islam, or at least one part of Islam, as an important defense mechanism against the commercialization of the world.

Peter Jennings

The Challenge of Islam

The expression *10/40 Window* has been often used by evangelical Christians, and even more frequently by evangelical missionaries, to refer to the sprawling region running east to west across the African and Asian continents that lies between the tenth and fortieth parallels. The area contains the largest population of non-Christians in the world. It reaches from ten degrees to forty degrees north of the equator and spans the globe all the way from North Africa across to China. But from the faith perspective, it is best known as an entrenched "window of resistance" to Christian missions and evangelism. In contrast to what Jenkins and others term the "Christian South," it is barren ground for church planters. It is a trackless desert of counter-Christianity.

Curiously, much, but not all, of Christian missions rhetoric about the 10/40 Window wittingly or unwittingly neglects to point out the obvious. The countries and cultures in this zone of resistance are predominantly Muslim. As the West's deepening crisis in its confrontation with radical Islam has made everyone painfully aware, Islam itself is not only resistant to evangelization but also frequently declares those who are converted from Islam to be apostates, subject to death and execution under Sharia, Islamic law based on the Qur'an. A much-publicized international incident in Afghanistan during the spring of 2006, when a Christian convert was condemned to death by an Islamic court, brought this fact to worldwide attention. Not only does traditional Islam—as opposed to an increasingly reticent and besieged "moderate" (read Westernized) Islam—declare its own sort of internal jihad against Christian conversion, it also rejects the presence of mission-oriented Christian communities within the Muslim transnational state, what classically was known as the *Dar al-Islam* (House of Submission), as a threat to a divinely ordained order of things.

The cherished claim of Western liberals that Islam has always supported a pluralistic, multireligious civil society, as demonstrated by medieval Spain, is a misleading historical simplism. Moorish Spain was never pluralistic in the Western sense. It was a stratified society where freedom of worship came at the expense of legal religious discrimination—what was called *dhimmitude*, after the Arabic word *dhimma* (tutelage)—that was really a form of faith-based apartheid. Furthermore, *dhimmitude* was extended only to Jews and Christians, or what the Qur'an calls the "People of the Book." Adherents of other religions, particularly Hindus when subjugated by Muslim armies, were given the option of conversion or death. Insofar as the Western value of religious pluralism to a significant extent has evolved from the otherworldly and pacifistic tendencies within historic Christianity, the notion of evangelizing Islamic cultures is more problematic than one can imagine.

In effect, the Christian theology of missions—whether old-guard or postmodern cum missional—has been unable to come to grips with the challenge of Islam. During the European Middle Ages, Islam quickly put Christendom on the military defensive, conquering much of what had been the post-Constantinian Roman lands. When Europe countered with the crusades from the twelfth through the fourteenth centuries, the previously disorganized and disintegrating Islamic Empire, split between the Fatimids in Egypt and the Abbasids in what is now Iraq, was reinvigorated and militarily reemboldened. For much of the fourteen-hundred-year seesaw struggle between the

West and Islam, there has been little attempt at understanding the profound differences between the two dominant Abrahamic faiths.

Even today, most conversation has focused on either demonizing the other or elaborating the naive and uninformed supposition that Islam can be easily absorbed into a secular, pluralist ecumene. It is becoming increasingly clear, despite a certain persistent myopia among the West's intellectual, political, and cultural elites, that a long-simmering clash of civilizations is taking place and that the West is engaged in a multifront war not with terrorism, which historically has been Christian in name as much as it has been Islamic, but with what scholars have come to term radical Islamism—the effort to foster a global Islamic state through revolutionary and sometimes violent means.

Like the Cold War, this conflict is not a black-and-white one; it is swathed in different shades of gray. Nor is it a full-pitched battle with distinct antagonists and a recognizable time line. There are war fronts that suddenly pop up around the world, then fade away. There are belligerent noises made that fade into the low chatter of diplomacy. Such was also the case a millennium earlier. Torrents of ink have been spilled lately, gathering steam since September 11, 2001, about the causes, prognoses, and sources of blame for this war. But the unassailable fact is that historically those peoples who have been predominantly Christian and Islamic have never been capable of anything more than a short-lived shotgun marriage to each other. During the colonial period the Western gunboats supplied the shotgun. Among the swelling ranks of Islamist legions throughout the old *Dar al-Islam*, the shotgun has been replaced by the roadside incendiary device or the suicide bomb pack.

What is the origin of this ever-deepening clash? In a profound sense we can attribute it to the irreconcilable differences between the Islamist vision and the West's, harking back to the advent of the new militant faith in the seventh century. The contest has overshadowed the history of civilization for the past millennium and a half with the exception of the years from about 1800 to 1990. Its antecedents are complex and the prognosis increasingly problematic. The old nostrums about properly managing conflict in the Middle East, particularly as they are framed from the standpoint of Western geopolitics, day by day seem to lose both their insightfulness and relevance. The clash of civilizations is eminently a clash of revelations, and it can be traced all the way back to the story of Abraham in the book of Genesis. While innumerable interfaith initiatives aimed at finding common ground among the three main Abrahamic religions abound in both liberal Protestant and Western academic circles, the efforts tend to be misguided, if not self-defeating.

Bernard Lewis, the eminent American academic authority on Islam and its relationship to the West, has written numerous books bringing this clash into focus. In the conclusion to his influential book *What Went Wrong?*—an attempt to analyze historically the current international situation as seen through Muslim eyes—Lewis makes three basic points: First, Muslims have a long and lasting historical memory, whereas Westerners have a very short one, if they are not historically ignorant. Second, unlike the West, which considers the last five hundred years to be an age of advance for individual liberty and human emancipation, the Muslim world has been in a funk. It has been boiling with resentment toward the gradual loss of its world supremacy and its humiliating subordination to European powers, values, and commercial interests. Third, many groups within Muslim civilization are increasingly itching for opportunities to settle scores and level the playing field. Because so much of the West—particularly the Balkans, Palestine, and Spain (which Muslims still call "Andalusia," its medieval name)—was once ruled by the Islamic caliphate, more militant Islamic visionaries with long memories and a determination to right perceived wrongs have slowly and steadily begun to envision some version of their own *reconquista*. Lewis notes trenchantly: "For Usama bin Laden and his circle, the prime and immediate cause of the present phase of the struggle is the American military presence in Arabia, . . . where the Qur'an brought God's final revelation to mankind, and where the first Muslim state was founded and ruled by the Prophet himself."[1]

However, this particular grievance and other local grievances—such as those found in Bosnia, Kosovo, Chechnya, and Kashmir—are actually a subset of what Lewis dubs "the overarching problem" in the minds of Muslims. The main problem is "the Western dominance over the whole Islamic world, which had been growing for centuries and crested in the twentieth century. For Usama bin Laden and those who share in his views—and there are many—the object of the struggle is the elimination of intrusive Western power and corrupting Western influence from all the lands of Islam, and the

---

1. Bernard Lewis, *What Went Wrong?* (New York: Oxford University Press, 2002), 204–5.

restoration of Islamic authenticity and authority in these lands. When this has been accomplished, the stage will be set for the final struggle to bring God's message to all mankind in all the world."[2]

Lewis chooses the slightly provocative term "the final struggle" to suggest a misty glimpse of what may be coming down the road. But as the events of the new millennium rapidly unfold, the implication is clear. Even if Westerners remain comfortably entranced with and self-absorbed in some version of the post-Cold War liberal and rose-colored picture of the international order, not as a clash of civilizations but as a clutch of negotiations, the signs are unmistakable, and they are also becoming ominous. Apocalyptic scenarios do not necessarily play out well in a postmodern, flat world, but we find ourselves increasingly in the shadow of a mood of "final struggle" that is projected in all three of the sacred texts of the Abrahamic religions. This sense of a coming end-times struggle is anchored profoundly in the three different traditions of revelation, which may be reconcilable at a superficial but not an ontological level. Revelation cannot be negotiated. It is either of God or not of God.

The Clash of Revelations

Let us begin with Abraham. Both Jews and Christians are familiar with the story in Genesis and, like Muslims, consider themselves to be Abraham's children. But the same genealogy is not necessarily the backbone of compatible eschatologies, and as the histories of revelations proceed, the chasm between the different religious interpretations of God's promise to his children becomes ever wider. If we read the book of Genesis "structurally"—as certain literary critics would say—as a text that is full of "dyads," or oppositional pairs, what at first seems unitary is ultimately riddled with difference. What appears smooth and continuous becomes jarring and conflicted. Scripture is all about God's guarantee of shalom (peace/wholeness). But it is just as much about those who "cry 'Peace, peace,' when there is no peace."[3]

God's promise to Abraham and Sarah that they will have a son from whom will spring a great nation has a false start in the birth of Ishmael

2. Ibid.
3. Cf. Jer. 6:14; 8:11.

through the slave-girl Hagar, the mother of the Bedouin and the beginning of the true lineage of the Muslims (according to their tradition). Later the promise is fulfilled in the arrival of Isaac, the progenitor of the Jewish people. Isaac's twin sons, Jacob and Esau, become in their own lifetime the archetypes of the saved and the damned: "'Was not Esau Jacob's brother?' the LORD says. 'Yet I have loved Jacob, but Esau I have hated'" (Mal. 1:2–3). These differences are exponentially magnified as the line between truth and deceit is firmly drawn, and as what the Bible calls "the day of the LORD" approaches.

From the Jewish and Christian angle, the differences are understated in the biblical text, but highly consequential. The divergence between the Islamic and the Judeo-Christian outlook can be located in Genesis 17, where God makes his "everlasting covenant" with Abraham, to whom he promises "the whole land of Canaan" in exchange for the latter's service and fidelity. As a seal, or sign, of the covenant, God tells Abraham that he and the males in his household are to be circumcised. From this moment onward, circumcision is intimately bound up with both divine call and election. "Any uncircumcised male," God declares, "who has not been circumcised in the flesh, will be cut off from his people" (Gen. 17:14).

At the heart of this covenantal relationship is God's promise that still another son besides Ishmael will be born. The frequent Sunday school interpretation of the birth of the two sons of Abraham is usually moralistic. In following the ancient Near Eastern custom of employing one's maidservant as a surrogate mother when the legal wife is childless, Abraham is assumed to have been impatient, to have relied on his own wisdom rather than taking God at his word, and to have failed to wait faithfully for the Lord to perform the miracle of providing a baby when both parents were far beyond the natural age for having a child. According to this interpretation, the fiasco with Hagar was proof positive that one must do things God's way. After Hagar conceived Ishmael, Sarah became jealous. She banished Hagar and Ishmael into the desert, whereupon God intervened and rescued the pitiable pair from certain death. In short, Abraham and Sarah blew it, and they had to wait a while before God made good on his intentions and did it right the second time around.

But this account misses some important nuances that appear in the biblical text itself. The key passage follows immediately upon God's warning about not heeding the requirement for circumcision. God says to Abraham regarding Sarah:

"I will bless her and she shall be the mother of nations; the kings of many people shall spring from her." Abraham threw himself down on his face; he laughed and said to himself, "Can a son be born to a man who is a hundred years old? Can Sarah bear a son when she is ninety?" He said to God, "If only Ishmael might live under thy special care!" But God replied, "No. Your wife Sarah shall bear you a son, and you shall call him Isaac. With him I will fulfill my covenant, an everlasting covenant with his descendants after him. I have heard your prayer for Ishmael. I have blessed him and will make him fruitful. I will multiply his descendants; he shall be father of twelve princes, and I will raise a great nation from him. But my covenant I will fulfill with Isaac, whom Sarah will bear to you at this season next year." (Gen. 17:16–21 NEB)

The story of Isaac is not so much about humans tempting the Lord and preventing the Lord from doing things his own way as it is about what later Christian theology would call special revelation as a warrant for a special destiny. The original promise to Abraham is that God will multiply his descendants and from them "raise a great nation." Here that original promise is extended to Ishmael. Powerful posterity is a perennial Bedouin dream, and Abraham—who was a wanderer and an alien in his land—was no different. But the promise to Abraham is now the promised land itself, which shall be fulfilled through Isaac, and Isaac alone. In other words, it is impossible to read the biblical text, which both orthodox Jews and evangelical Christians regard with absolute authority, in any other way: by his "word" God gives the land to the people who would later be known as the Jews. Both Ishmael and Isaac are "blessed." But only Isaac receives the unique blessing of the land, indistinguishable from the covenant itself.

The dispute over whether the territory the Romans named "Palestine" rightly belongs to Jews or Muslims is the one nonnegotiable sticking point in the never-ending Middle Eastern conflict. The point does not require discussion. For all the dramatic Western hand-wringing and litany of Muslim grievances that have been officially articulated since 1948, when the State of Israel was recognized by the United Nations, the argument ultimately comes down to a profound issue of theology: whose revelation is right? The dispute is not really about ancient territorial claims and historical precedent. If that set of criteria would be taken seriously, as it has been in settlement of American Indian land claims vis-à-vis the United States government, justice would without doubt be on the side of the Israelis.

Nor does it come down to the oft-repeated charge that the forma-tion of Israel represents a colonialist intrusion on some prior Arab sovereignty or the displacement by European settlers of a preexist-ing Muslim nation. Palestine was never a nation. Throughout most of the previous fifteen hundred years, it was always a province of succeeding transnational Islamic empires, which is precisely why the creation of the State of Israel has inflicted such a wound in the Islamic consciousness. The last time it was a sovereign nation, before the formation of the State of Israel in 1948, occurred during the brief Maccabean period preceding the takeover by Rome in 63 BC. In other words, as a nation-state per se, it has always been Jewish.

The offense of the dominant Jewish presence and Jewish state-hood in Palestine can neither be comprehended nor appeased by reliance on the usual methods of arbitration that have prevailed in Western jurisprudence since bygone times. Arbitration can be seri-ously entertained as viable only if both sides adhere to a worldview that supports such negotiation, with the meld of Roman, Germanic, and English law that constitutes Western legal practice, moral values, and standards of human rights. Increasingly, both sides do not.

As we have seen, the most visible and obvious manifestation of the global resurgence of religion is the rise of an ever-potent Islamism, fueled not only by oil wealth and a renewed Muslim self-confidence in the face of never-ending waffling on the part of the world's politi-cians, diplomats, and pundits, but also by the fundamental force of Muhammad's teachings around the globe. And we can sum up that force with the statement every student learns in any introductory course on world religions: the Qur'an is God's absolute and final revelation, superseding both the old covenant of the Jews and the new covenant of Christians.

There is no possibility of interpreting exactly what the Qur'an might mean, as both Jewish and Christian scholars have for eons been doing with the Bible. As Jenkins observes, Muslims

see Muhammad as the last and greatest of prophets. . . . Islam, even in its most liberal forms, scarcely allows for neutrality. A Christian well-wisher might praise the "Prophet Muhammad" and believe that he was in some sense inspired by God, making the Qur'an a magnifi-cent spiritual document that has spawned one of the world's great faiths. But that is nowhere near enough for Muslims, who believe that Muhammad himself had precisely no input or role in the making

of the Qur'an, which was divinely dictated through angelic mediation. For a Muslim, it is a deadly falsehood to say that Muhammad
founded a religion: Islam is as old as the Creation, and Adam, Jesus,
and Moses were Muslims.[4]

The only problem for Muslims is how to apply the general terms of
this final revelation, which the Qur'an represents, to the practicalities
and conundrums of everyday life in the way that district courts in
America specify the implications of the US Constitution. Islamic
interpretation is always legal interpretation. There is no Pauline
struggle between the spirit and the letter, except in certain now-
heterodox sects of Islam, such as Sufism, which are not generally
recognized by Muslim clergy and historically have at times been
persecuted. The letter is what counts.

The Qur'an is not a covenant at all in the sense of the assurance
of a faithful relationship between God and the believer that calls for
steadfastness and endurance, even when God's ultimate ways are not
known. It is instead a presumed declaration by God himself, Muslims
believe, of what is the case and what is not the case in every aspect
of life. About that which the Qur'an does not specifically speak, the
hadith offer guidance. The hadith are the traditions concerning what
the Prophet himself said and did. They are supplemented by the standard practices of *qiyas* (the use of analogy in reasoning) and *ijma* (the
consensus of the community), yielding the complex and long-evolving
system of judicial interpretation about everything from female dress to
the conduct of war. This system is know as Sharia, or Islamic law.

The Meaning of Israel

Islamists, even the most militant variants of them that include
Osama bin Laden, are often dismissed in the Western press and in
popular discourse as violent terrorists without a clear or coherent
religious vision that somehow can be accommodated to Western
expectations about how religious people are supposed to think,
talk, and conduct themselves. But Islamists simply comprise the
radical end of a spectrum that has no clear breaks within the
historic Islamic tradition itself. That explains why radical figures

4. Philip Jenkins, *God's Continent: Christianity, Islam, and Europe's Religious Crisis* (New York: Oxford University Press, 2007), 267.

such as bin Laden, and more recently Hassan Nasrallah of Hez-
bollah, can command far more prestige among the disaffected
Muslim masses than Westerners find plausible. The usual Western
academic parsing of the distinction between "Islam," "radical
Islam," and "Islamism" (which is supposedly incompatible with
liberal, secular democracy), or between "genuine Islam" and the
"extremists," is proving to be quite unhelpful. Increasingly many
Muslims themselves resent the attempt because it seeks to define
Islam solely on the basis of what the Western secular elites deem
acceptable and unacceptable. The same sort of bias is evident in
the United States and also in the developing world when some
people dismiss others with strong faith commitments, who have
more traditional social values and simplistic readings of the Bible,
as fundamentalists.

A different picture emerges if one looks beyond the world media
statements that bin Laden has made since 2001, designed strictly
for propaganda purposes, and examines his actual writings and
interviews, many of which have been translated and compiled in
recent years. We find the portrait of a thoughtful and learned man,
who though militant and without doubt extreme even by pious or
conventional Muslim standards, has leveraged connections, money,
organizational abilities, personal charisma, bravado, and polemical
gifts to mobilize the aspirations of a new breed of young Muslims
in diverse types of global Islamic culture and contexts. That does
not excuse him or mitigate the overwhelming threat he and his ilk
pose to the West. After all, Hitler had many of the same qualities,
as probably did Genghis Khan.

What Westerners miss in bin Laden's rhetoric is that he pitches his
radical Islamism not to fellow true believers, as we would phrase it in
the West, but to the *umma*—the Arabic word for the global Muslim
community—of which he sees himself the true, legitimate leader.
The idea of Islam as a planetary *umma*, as opposed to a system of
religious and political practice seeking ascendancy within the existing
Western-dominated and Western-derived world order, is not trifling.
The new postmodern Islamist *umma* transcends, overcomes, and
absorbs the corrupt social, political, and moral—read Western and
modern—order that has spread from West to East for centuries. It
is the new and expanding present-day *Dar al-Islam* that is without
borders or national distinctions. If Hitler said something like "Today
Germany, tomorrow the world," a synopsis of bin Laden's messages

might read as follows: "Today the purification of Islam, tomorrow the purification of the world."

The question of Israel—what Muslims habitually dub the "Palestine" question—is for that reason not simply a political question. It precedes all other questions, because it is central to the problem of the present and future *umma* as the concrete realization within time and space of God's absolute revealed will and truth. The question of Israel is pivotal to the clash of civilizations because its current historical struggle makes plain the clash of revelations. As Muslims are desecularized and more susceptible to the exhortations of the Islamists, this fact does not escape them, whereas it continues to escape Westerners, who still peer at world crises through the glass of modernist rationalism and post-Enlightenment liberalism.

It is not incidental that when bin Laden began making his public statements for a global audience in 1994, he focused on the question of Israel. "The Betrayal of Palestine" was composed as a public letter to Abd-al-Aziz ibn Abd Allah ibn Baaz, Grand Mufti of Saudi Arabia from 1993 to 1999; the letter was released on December 29, 1994. The Saudi kingdom officials had already stripped bin Laden of his Saudi citizenship in the spring of that year. Although bin Laden shows outrage in the letter for the introduction of Western troops into Saudi Arabia, what he calls the "Land of the Two Holy Sanctuaries," he is even more incensed by the signing of the Oslo Accords, inked in the summer of 1993, that for a brief time promised the resolution of the seemingly intractable Israeli–Palestinian conflict. Baaz's endorsement of the Accords at the behest of the Saudi government was the premier focus of bin Laden's wrath in the letter. A noteworthy sidelight of the letter is bin Laden's unvarnished attempt to establish his own credentials as a religious authority, even if he is not a cleric per se.

Bin Laden upbraids Baaz for "abandoning" the Saudi shrines to "the Crusader-Jewish forces of occupation" and for "conferring legitimacy on the contracts of surrender to the Jews that were signed by the traitorous and cowardly Arab tyrants." He continues: "The current Jewish enemy is not an enemy settled in his own original country fighting its defense until he gains a peace agreement, but an attacking enemy and a corrupter of religion and the world." The "legal duty regarding Palestine . . . is to wage *jihad* for the sake of God, and to motivate our *umma* to *jihad* so that Palestine may be completely liberated and returned to Islamic sovereignty."[5] Referring specifically to the Oslo Accords, which he describes as "documents of capitulation and surrender of the Holy City of Jerusalem and all of Palestine to the Jews" as well as "their acknowledgment of Jewish sovereignty over Palestine for ever," bin Laden declaims that "this alleged peace that the rulers and tyrants are falling over themselves to make with the Jews is nothing but a massive betrayal."[6]

Bin Laden became known to the world after the bombings of US embassies in 1998 and achieved the status of an archvillain following the attack on the Twin Towers three years later. Since those events, the Western media has conveyed the common view that the ultimate offense of America has been its support of Israel politically and its huge presence through military deployments and oil contracts throughout the Middle East. The implication again is that underneath it all the clash is just a territorial or cultural dispute, or a combination of the two. As the apologists for Islamism these days are accustomed to reiterating, if the West would just respect the Muslim world more, the conflict would abate. For bin Laden, and what he perhaps with slightly less exaggeration than one would care to admit calls his "1.5 billion followers," there can be no compromise or mutual respect.

In a December 1998 interview with Al-Jazeera, the Arab world's counterpart to CNN, bin Laden overtly and proudly asserted: "Every Muslim, from the moment they realize the distinction in their hearts, hates Americans, hates Jews, and hates Christians. This is a part of our belief and our religion."[7] If the sentiment were not already shared by many, bin Laden—always the consummate politician and propagandist—could not have said it casually on Al-Jazeera and gotten away with it without appearing to be a lunatic or a madman in the eyes of the clientele he was even then cultivating.

When asked pointedly about the now-familiar conspiracy theory that the CIA both created and funded him during the 1980s war in Afghanistan against the Soviet Union, bin Laden picks no bones. He compares Muslim collaboration with the Americans against the Soviets to the seventh-century alliance between the Muslims and Per-

5. Bruce Lawrence, ed., *Messages to the World: The Statements of Osama bin Laden* (London: Verso, 2005), 9.

6. Ibid., 10.

7. Ibid., 87.

sians against the Byzantines (Christians). "Fighting the Byzantines was a duty, but after their victories over the Byzantines . . . they set about fighting the Persians," whom they ultimately conquered and converted to Islam. All the while and with whomever he makes alliances, bin Laden says, he is in the business of "supporting Islam" and the still-unrequited dream of a global *Dar al-Islam*, where Sharia will not be a provincial religious law but a universal one. "Unintended confluence of interests does not mean there is any kind of link or tacit agreement. We have been advancing since those days [of the original Islamic expansion] and . . . have been spreading our message for more than twelve years on the duty of boycotting American goods, attacking its military forces and its economy."[8]

The matter of Israel, the "Little Satan," as Ayatollah Khomeini would have termed it, and the matter of the power of the West, led by the "Great Satan" America, are thus inextricably fused together. Hitler sought to eliminate the "germ" of Judaism from what he considered to be a pure global Aryan *Volk*, to be followed up by the subjugation and eventual elimination of the "undermen" (*Untermenschen*), or nonwhite races. The more extreme fascist denomination of Islamism strives for the elimination first of Jewish sovereignty, then of Christians from the pure global *umma*, followed by the forced conversion or ultimate elimination of what Sayyid Qutb, the ideological architect of jihadism and spiritual forerunner of bin Laden, dubbed the "*jahiliyyists*," or secularists. The Koranic word *jahiliyya* means the state of polytheism, individualism, blindness, or ignorance that preceded the imposition of Islam on the Arabian peninsula. The term *jahiliyya* can be easily construed, if one peruses contemporary jihadists' Web sites, to mean basically everything associated with Western liberal democracy and its intellectual legacy.

The Weakness of Western Christianity

In the final analysis, Islam's collision with the West amounts to the question of right revelation, as we have insisted, and these now-familiar global culture wars become subordinate to the larger concern of whether it is biblical truth or Qur'anic truth that informs and guides values, institutions, and events. The clash of

8. Ibid., 88.

civilizations is not between cultural heritages as much as it is between two resurgent faiths. The battlefield on which the clash is already taking place is not the 10/40 Window but the global media. It is a clash of convictions, where Christians increasingly are outgunned.

The Western evangelical church, in contrast to its counterpart in the global South, has had a fatal attraction to contemporary consumer culture and made a fateful alliance with it. The attraction is not unlike the one the people and kings of ancient Israel had with the Asherahs (hā'ǎšērôt) and the Baals (habĕ'ālîm). Like ancient Israel's subtle entanglement with the local pagan cults, many evangelical Christians, including many postmodern adherents, have seen the power of the gospel dwindle in their lives and their churches because they have gone whoring after the false gods of spiritual and material consumption. Just as the ancient worshipers at Jewish shrines could not differentiate between worship of the one God of Abraham, Isaac, and Jacob and local fertility rites, contemporary Christians frequently fail to distinguish between worship as self-surrender and as self-gratification.

The Islamists know that the West is entangled with this cult of consumption, and they have gone out of their way to denounce it and to demand its overthrow in the name of the "one true God" of Islam. A widely circulated story tells how radical Islamism was birthed. As a young educational bureaucrat for the Egyptian government in the early 1950s, Qutb was sent on a fact-finding mission to America to learn about Western ways and mores. He witnessed and was supposedly shocked by what he considered sexual licentiousness in America, exemplified in teenage pop culture, dating customs, and casual gender relations. According to the story, such outrage prompted him to begin formulating a program for a revival of Islam as a counterforce to the Westernization and secularization that was sweeping the Middle East.

The lore concerning Qutb is instructive only because in a perverse sense it points up what should be more obvious than it has been so far to those who lament the de-Christianization of the West. The issue is not simply gender relations. It is also the question the prophet Elijah raised when confronted with the massive confusion in his time between worship of the Holy One of Israel and the cults of the Baals: Who really is God in Israel? Like Elijah, we need to ask: Who really is God these days in the West?

In the West, Christians themselves cannot be a counterforce to the trend toward radical Islamism in the 10/40 Window unless they come to terms with their own spiritual weakness and the way the gospel has been compromised for the sake of the greatest of all consumerist idols—"relevance," whatever that might mean, as well as "church growth." If Christians are going to contend with radical Islamism, they are going to have to reinvent themselves in a more powerful and positive manner than they have ever conceived, in the way Jesus called for when he proclaimed the Great Commission. There is a vast difference—indeed, to borrow a phrase from Søren Kierkegaard, an "infinite, qualitative difference"—between consumerism and the strategies of incarnational ministry. One can be wholly relevant without succumbing to the cult of relevance. That is what the concept of indigenization implies.

As Olivier Roy points out, something akin, but not equivalent, to indigenization is happening globally in Islam. The struggle to define the relationship between faith and culture at a global level cuts across religious borders. "What is new in Western Islam," Roy writes, "is the crisis of cultural reference in itself. Practicing Muslims are embroiled in a struggle less to promote a minority culture against a dominant one than to define their own relationship with the very concept of culture."[9] Globalization, or more specifically the globo-electro-Western culture that high-tech communications has spawned, has affected every form of monotheistic absolutism. Just as these systems of communication have engendered a true, deculturated, global *corpus Christi* that has become indigenized in myriad contexts and hence decoupled from the West, they have also conjured up a global but deterritorialized *umma*.

The Western mosque is the premier illustration for this point. According to Roy, "The lives of the leaders of many such mosques have followed a 'deterritorialized' trajectory. . . . Young converts can travel throughout Europe, going from one such mosque to another, ignoring ethnic divides and speaking English everywhere (just as Catholic clerics and monks in the Middle Ages, going from one monastery to the other, spoke Latin)." Although *jihad* is both an essential Qur'anic and a classical Muslim concept, globalization has given it an entirely new twist because religious commitment

9. Olivier Roy, *Globalized Islam: The Search for a New Ummah* (New York: Columbia University Press, 2004), 121.

no longer needs to be unraveled from a particular set of cultural identities and loyalties. The majority of the radical "preachers and organizations target second-generation Muslims, explicitly playing on their sense of being victims of racism, exclusion and loneliness in the West, and hence are very successful among Blacks or non-Muslim members of the underclass, . . . members of the vanguard of internationalist jihadists who fight the global superpower and the international system."[10]

In other words, indigenization is not a process that instantiates a general form of revelation in a specific cultural situation, the so-called global-local (glocal) scene. Globalized religion is at the same time indigenized religion, except that religion is indigenized in the transnational, or transcultural, context itself. The sense of exclusion, which affects all immigrants and many of the new cultural nomads in a world without borders, is not alone an explanation for the sudden rise and unprecedented fury of jihadism. We must take account of the motivating force of jihadism itself, and that is something Western secularists appear chronically incapable of grasping.

Consider a statement by leading French intellectuals in February 2006 regarding a threat by an Islamist activist to kill controversial writer Salman Rushdie for "debasing Islam" and the so-called cartoon controversy in the Western press, when a Danish newspaper published unflattering pictures of the prophet Muhammad and Muslim mobs around the world threatened violence against the authors of the caricatures. Many of those signing the statement were Muslim. The statement reads as follows:

> After having overcome fascism, Nazism, and Stalinism, the world now faces a new totalitarian global threat: Islamism. We, writers, journalists, intellectuals, call for resistance to religious totalitarianism and for the promotion of freedom, equal opportunity, and secular values for all. The recent events, which occurred after the publication of drawings of Muhammad in European newspapers, have revealed the necessity of the struggle for these universal values. . . . It is not a clash of civilizations nor an antagonism of West and East that we are witnessing, but a global struggle that confronts democrats and theocrats. . . . Islamism is a reactionary ideology, which kills equality, freedom, and secularism wherever it is present. Its success can only lead to a world of domination: man's domination of woman, the Islamists' domina-

10. Ibid., 309.

tion of all the others. To counter this, we must assure universal rights
to oppressed or discriminated people . . . so that a critical spirit may
be exercised on all continents, against all abuses and all dogmas. We
appeal to democrats and free spirits of all countries that our century
should be one of Enlightenment, not of obscurantism.[11]

There is something incredibly naive, though painfully recognizable, in this well-intentioned statement on the part of the French
intellectual left. The explosion of the Rushdie affair once more in
2007 underscored this point all the more. In its presumption that
the battle against radical Islamism will be ideological, the statement
implies that the struggle is between political libertarianism and
totalitarianism. Such constructions would have been appropriate
if one were dealing with the sort of historic totalitarianism that
France encountered in the 1930s, particularly the Nazi variety. It is
telling that the statement challenges cultural relativism, but it does
so in the name of the rationalism and universalism of the French
Enlightenment, which has been the staple of Gallic intellectual life
for almost three centuries.

What the statement so glaringly misses is the context surrounding the recrudescence of Islamist authoritarianism: the postmodern
West's failure to come to terms with the resurgent religion of Islam.
It has been said that if "fundamentalism" means the attention and
strict adherence to all minutiae of the Qur'an, then all Muslims
by definition are fundamentalists. The Qur'an does not require a
doctrine of inerrancy to warrant the belief that it is completely ap-
plicable in every detail to every bit of life's minutiae. In his major
tome *Social Justice in Islam*, Qutb put it this way: Islam "enunci-
ates for me a complete theory of life." This theory is "not open to
modification or to adulteration, either in its fundamentals or in its
general aims." In order for this "complete theory to bear its full
natural fruits, it is necessary to make a complete application of it.
Otherwise, even the slightest change in its fundamentals or aims
will produce a disorder, because it will no longer be in conformity
with the Islamic conception of life."[12]

11. The Editors, "Confronting Islamist Totalitarianism," *The Middle Eastern Quar-
terly* 13 (Summer 2006), http://www.meforum.org/article/998, with the statement signed
by Salman Rushdie, Bernard-Henri Levy, Caroline Fourest, et al.

12. Sayyid Qutb, *Social Justice in Islam*, trans. John B. Hardie (Oneonta, NY: Islamic
Publications International, 2000), 284.

Although Qutb obviously does not speak for the whole of histori-cal Islam, or even for a sizable fraction of it, his language is clearly totalitarian in its implications. One could easily substitute the word "Aryan" for "Islamic" in Qutb's text and confuse it with a typical piece of Nazi apologetics during the Third Reich. Just as Nazism and fascism derived their theories from the pseudo-doctrines of ethnic and racial nationalism prevalent in Europe during the nineteenth century, so Qutb's Islamism constitutes a totalizing of tendencies already inherent in early twentieth-century religious rhetoric com-mon among anticolonial radicals of the period.

In Qutb we find a nonnegotiable hostility toward the West. "There is this deep-seated and inherited hostility to Islam in the European nature itself," he writes. "The European mentality is rooted in ma-terial foundations, and the influence of intellectual and spiritual interests is weak; such has been the case from the time of Roman civilization to the present day."[13] Qutb argues that Western civiliza-tion as a whole is "Roman" and not "Christian." Whereas the latter is founded on a system of unconditional and monotheistic truth, the former rests on a view of life as "a matter of advantage, quite independent of absolute values."[14] This sort of talk has a remarkable affinity with how Nazi propaganda portrayed the Jew in contrast to the "pure" or native spirituality of the Aryan. According to Nazi polemics, the Jew by nature was self-centered, individualistic, ma-terialistic, and devoid of the folkish virtue of sympathy for one's fellow humans.

Like the German fascists, Qutb also argues that the spirit of Islam is embedded in an ancestral identity. Because Westerners are de facto Germanic peoples linguistically bound in their destiny to the history of "Romanness," their purpose in history can never be reconciled with that of Islamic Semitism. Islam must overcome the West before the West overcomes Islam. And the times are shifting in Islam's favor. "The tide of Islam has commenced to rise," Qutb wrote in the early 1950s.[15] Muslims must hope in the future for the "control of the Western world."[16] Muslim "universalism" is in reality reserved for all non-European peoples. Qutb refers metaphorically

13. Ibid., 279.
14. Ibid., 281.
15. Ibid., 276.
16. Ibid., 277.

to all Western thought and culture, including the Communism of his day, which was at its high-water mark, as a series of "caravans" traversing and violating sacred Muslim space. If the source of the caravan forays is not eliminated, Islam can never assert its rightful and God-ordained role of global spiritual and political dominion.

Qutb, unlike his liberal Western counterparts, recognizes that what remains ultimately at stake is a clash of revelations. But he is contemptuous of the Christian alternative. Christianity is "ascetic" and "weak," he proclaims. Following Friedrich Nietzsche's cue in *The Genealogy of Morals* and *The Antichrist*, Qutb glorifies Islam as a kind of warrior faith in comparison with Christianity's servility, what the German philosopher termed its "transvaluation" of the martial ethic into a "slave morality." "Islam is essentially different from Christianity," according to Qutb. "It commands the fostering of material powers, it enjoins resistance and struggle in war, and it warns the weaklings who tamely submit that theirs will be an evil fate in this world and in the next."[17] These words sound the familiar and classic language of European totalitarianism. Interestingly, Qutb embellishes this statement with a string of four key passages from the Qur'an in their entirety. "Islam's supreme virtue is that it preserves the unity of life and that it makes no distinction between means and ends."[18] This lack of distinction again mirrors the discourse of totalitarianism, which has repeatedly and almost unstintingly used such a justification for the gross violation of international protocols, agreements, and civil rights.

But what has in the past been termed "fascism," or "totalitarianism" (whatever the unquestionably negative connotation of those terms), did not erupt gratuitously or without reason from the cracks and fissures of history. In the West were many liberal defenders of even Nazism when it first became prominent in Germany during the early 1930s. Was not Nazism a legitimate response to the stupidity and injustices wrought by the victorious allies following World War I in their vendetta against Germany and in their excessive reparations policies? That question was posed repeatedly as late as 1935 by many so-called progressives, who were soured by the economic collapse and small-mindedness of the Western democracies. Is not Islamism, despite its incompatibility with all contemporary liberal values, an

17. Ibid., 273–74.
18. Ibid., 283.

understandable reaction against the global overreach of the pax Americana? Thus proclaim today's self-critical Western elites.

But this analysis is dangerously wrongheaded. The revenge theory of history accounts for the ideological sources of violent political movements, but it does not explain why these movements become expansive and totalistic over time. In their introduction to the book *Islam, Globalization, and Postmodernity*, two authors, one of whom is Muslim, give an interesting description, with not a little poetic irony, of the recent antecedents of the current Islamic militancy against the West. Akbar Ahmed and Hastings Donnan maintain that since the fall of Communism, many Western political gestures aimed at the liberation of Muslim peoples from their oppressors—specifically, the Gulf War and the NATO intervention in Bosnia—have had the opposite psychological effect in the Middle East.[19] They have only served to galvanize a powerful sense of Muslim identity in opposition to the West. Thus the familiar criticism that the Iraq War has created more terrorists while failing to bring democracy to the Middle East may have to be construed in a broader context. Much of the critical rhetoric assumes that it is a specific war and a particular set of policies that has somehow undermined what would otherwise remain a modus vivendi between Islam and the West.

But Ahmed and Donnan, writing almost a decade before the attack on the Twin Towers and even several years before the first appearance of al-Qaida on the global scene, make it clear from a pro-Muslim perspective that the problem comes down to a true clash of civilizations. No matter what Western politicians—conservative or liberal—aim to do in liberating Muslims from their perceived global oppressors, there is going to be increasing blowback on the liberators. It is a no-win situation for the West unless Westerners accept the implicit premise behind the polemics of an increasingly radicalized Muslim *umma*—that emancipation for the Muslim world is equivalent to Islamization, a proposition that even the most left-leaning secular progressives would resist.

Ahmed and Donnan observe that the development of a "literate high culture" driving emancipation from oppressive "ancient regimes" has taken the historical form of secularism in the West and what we now term Islamism throughout Muslim civilization.

19. Akbar S. Ahmed and Hastings Donnan, "Islam in the Age of Postmodernity," in *Islam, Globalization, and Postmodernity* (London: Routledge, 1994), 1–20.

According to these authors, we can see this trend as a triumph of the "sacred" over the "profane" in world history. "The strength of Islam," they contend,

> lies not merely in its unambiguous, unbowdlerized commitment to a firmly delineated divine message, providing through its rules for social life a sustained handrail in the conduct of life, but also in the fact that, though it firmly regulates daily life, it does not sacralize it. Marxist societies, committed to a soteriology promising that *this* life will now be noble, could not cope with the squalid reality of "real socialism." Islam may be socially demanding but it does not abolish the dualism, which saves the sacred from being compromised by the profane.[20]

One of the main reasons that the 10/40 Window has acquired the status for which it is known in evangelical circles is the unprecedented power of Islam as a transcendental ideology in confronting the West. Western secularists have not yet figured out that Islam has more allure among the perceived victims of globalization and Westernization than anything they might offer up because it provides a collectivist vision that is also deeply spiritual. Evangelicals, in contrast, have tended to hang on to the old colonial mentality, which regards Muslims as on the same level as tribal animists or folk religionists rather than acknowledging Islam as a redoubtable force that at one time almost completely overwhelmed—and in the right circumstances could still overwhelm—the Christian West.

The only way Christianity can hope to succeed against Islam in today's global context is to put aside the secularist project altogether. That is not to say that Christianity must realign itself with what survives of the reactionary feudalism against which Marxism once rallied its troops, or must adopt some form of quasi-Marxist liberation theology in answer to Islam, which turns out to be just as nonsensical. Christianity today must become far more radical than it has ever imagined.

In this connection we can cite Augustine of Hippo, who some interpreters regard as the first postmodernist. He looked forward to the eventual triumph of GloboChristianity. Although he famously identified his "city of God" with the institutional church of his day, he was not a postmillennialist—one who sees the visible church as an

20. Ibid., xiv.

active advocate and administrator of divine justice in the world—in the modern sense. Most significantly, Augustine saw human history as a fierce spiritual struggle that often manifests itself in the social and political realm, a view that is uncannily similar to the classic Muslim take on jihad, as opposed to the contemporary Islamist understanding. Jihad literally means "struggle," and Muslim theologians historically have regarded the interior spiritual struggle (the greater jihad) as ultimately more important than the political and military one (the lesser jihad). Augustine professes that the struggle will go on until the end of time. "Better war with the hope of everlasting peace than slavery without any thought of liberation."[21]

Though we do not need to conceive of a Christian jihad, mainly because it would be instantly misconstrued, Augustine's point is something of which Christians need to remind themselves. The fulfillment of the Great Commission will not be without struggle. The struggle is ultimately a spiritual one, but it is real, it is contemporary, and it will become more intense as the years wear on. Through dialogue, Muslims and Christians may come to agree on common points of their mutual Abrahamic faiths, but the differences will always outweigh the similarities. The differences make the difference. Islam is founded on an absolutely objectivist revelation that we either accept or reject. Christianity is founded on a revelation in the person of Jesus, to whom we give the whole of our life and being. We can and should accept Muslims as divinely created and cared-for persons made in the image of God, with whom we can have loving and respectful relationships, but our agreement with them can only be relational, not in any way theological. We are engaged not so much in a struggle for the doctrinal truth of our faith as in a struggle to manifest the presence of Christ in what we know as the radical relationality that is at the heart of our commitment to the One who gave his life for each of us and for others—the One who says, "I am the truth," the One who is the way into the truth. To him we pledge our "troth," from which the word "truth" is derived. We pledge our allegiance to him and to him alone.

21. Augustine of Hippo, *Concerning the City of God*, trans. Henry Bettenson (New York: Penguin Books, 1972), 993 (21.15).

5

Radical Relationality

The Church in the Postmodern Cosmopolis

> God loves each of us as if there were only one of us.
>
> Augustine of Hippo

Toward a Reinvented Global Evangelicalism

What would a reinvented, postmodern, global evangelical Christianity look like in broad outline? The four R's of becoming a Christ-follower heeding the call of the Great Commission in a globopomo cosmopolis are as follows: radical, relational, revelatory, and rhizomic.

Radical. The word *radical* commonly connotes "extremist," or taking extreme action or an extreme position. Jesus certainly was a radical so far as this use of the word goes. But more important, Jesus was a radical because his extremism stemmed from a fundamental, or "root" (as the Latin *radix*, or *radicalis*, suggests), commitment to what God had revealed in his word, or instruction (torah), to his people.

When Jesus explained the so-called Great Commandment, he was exemplifying what it means to be both a Jewish and a Christian radical. "Hearing that Jesus had silenced the Sadducees, the

Pharisees got together. One of them, an expert in the law, tested him with this question: 'Teacher, which is the greatest commandment in the Law?' Jesus replied: ' "Love the Lord your God with all your heart and with all your soul and with all your mind." This is the first and greatest commandment. And the second is like it: "Love your neighbor as yourself." All the Law and the Prophets hang on these two commandments'" (Matt. 22:34–40).

The evangelist's employment of the Greek verb *krematai* (hang, depend) in the last sentence is significant. Not only is it used in various passages of the New Testament to describe Jesus "hanging" on the cross but it also has the figurative meaning of something large that is "held up" by something smaller or less visible, such as a door hanging on its hinges. Theologically, the cross is the fulcrum of everything that matters in following Christ (i.e., "take up your cross") because it signifies in a most radical fashion what God is all about. God so loved the world that he gave his only Son as a sacrificial love offering. Another means of expressing this insight would be to say that all the outward forms of revelation—the Law and the Prophets—derive from the love that God has always shown toward us and the love that we are commanded to show toward him in return.

Everything Jesus taught and exhibited through his deeds and sayings was to make this point manifest. In that respect Jesus's extreme actions were to expose the root of all authentic religious language and behavior.

Relational. If radical Christianity is about the love of God and the love of neighbor, then it is also relational. "Relationality" has become something of a catchphrase in postmodernist parlance. But that is only because it strikes at the heart of the Christian message. What we say and what we really mean—language and intentionality—have always been the crux of philosophical and theological inquiry since the ancient Greeks. Words and the correct deployment of words in language have been perennially fascinating to Western philosophers. It can be first found in Plato's *Cratylus,* which readers until recently presumed was a kind of prototext in the philosophy of language, but which many interpreters nowadays regard as a statement that truth is not dependent on "mere words."[1]

---

1. See Simon Keller, "An Interpretation of Plato's *Cratylus," Phronesis* 45 (November 2000): 284–305.

But Jesus did not care so much about correct formulation of the truth, nor about the objective reality corresponding to the formulation, as he did about the motive behind the formulation. Hence his relentless condemnation of the Pharisees as "hypocrites" (literally, those who judge only by external appearances or verbal testimony). So much of the tiresome and mindless critique of the straw man known as "postmodernism" by so-called evangelical defenders of the true Christian faith misses Jesus's own approach. It also overlooks his condemnation of those obsessed with formal consistency in their utterances and behavior rather than an attitude of surrender toward God and *agapē* toward others.

Jesus contextualized! He did not give a scrupulous argument for some theological position or interpretation he had chosen to defend against other "lawyers" or gentile opponents. Jesus contextualized because he came to reveal the Father.[2] Jesus revealed the Father in his teachings, which were always contextualized in terms of his relational dealings with others, especially those who were neither morally nor doctrinally pure—prostitutes, tax collectors, and thieves, as well as the unlearned and unwashed. From a Christian standpoint, as I have written elsewhere, the "real" is always relational, and the relational is the genuine *ens realissium* (final goal), the most real aspect of religious reality. There is no such thing as a Christian truth that stands by itself in some self-contained universe of Platonic ideas or in independent "logical space," as the twentieth-century philosopher Ludwig Wittgenstein termed it. Even the first Christian "apologists," such as Justin Martyr, were not technical philosophers or debate-team contestants. The Greek word *apologia* means a formal reply to one who has made a false accusation. The aim of the apologist was to show that Christians were not the ignorant degenerates that the common pagan libel had made them out to be but instead were authentic contributors to Roman society as well as what we would now call "good citizens."

As Christians we are called to reveal who Christ is—the truth of God made flesh in relation to us, the real Emmanuel, "God with us"—just as Christ revealed the Father. In every day and every way, the Christian life amounts to a radical relationality, a readiness to

2. "All things have been committed to me by my Father. No one knows who the Son is except the Father, and no one knows who the Father is except the Son and those to whom the Son chooses to reveal him" (Luke 10:22).

reveal who God is while "being Jesus" to others when the occasion arises. As Christians we are always Christs to one another.

Revelatory. Modernist critics of the latest youth-oriented "cooler than cool" sort of cultural postmodernism, which habitually calls itself the "new kind" of Christianity when it is no more than warmed-over 1960s-style social liberalism do have a point—everything else notwithstanding—that needs to be made. "Mere Christianity" can no more be identified with a simple antidogmatism, or antiauthoritarianism, or even a "generous orthodoxy," than can genuine and passionate love be defined as a simple recoil against hatred or indifference. So much of the American evangelical conversation has come to be framed in terms of how open-minded or nonjudgmental a Christian is supposed to be.

This conversation, which often dissipates into a nasty argument, represents little more than a form of internecine warfare among competing clans of the spiritually prideful. "Holier than thou" is thus postmodernized as "Less rigid than thou." Jesus never made a case for or against tolerance. He called sinners to repentance and the proud to humility. The very notion of repentance flies in the face of politically correct Christian pluralists who confuse the gospel with customer satisfaction. A decade or two ago there was a famous commercial promoting Burger King with the catchy slogan "Have it your way." We may dismiss so much of contemporary church experience as "Burger King Christianity" in this sense. Repentance does not necessarily entail an objective standard of Christian moral truth, as modernists claim, but neither does it ignore the infinite spiritual touchstone of God's formidable truth while implying a largely subjective standpoint of private, experiential testing, as today's pluralists presuppose. Thus a pastor (who shall go nameless) once marvelously said during a sermon, "Repentance is seeing oneself from God's point of view."

As religious historian Alan Wolfe has made clear, American Christianity in the last generation or so has been extensively "transformed" by global consumerism. Doctrinal or institutional tests of faith, except among denominationally minded pedants, have become for the most part irrelevant.[3] A broad-ranging experientialism—where the truth of faith is routinely validated merely in terms of the emo-

---

3. See Alan Wolfe, *The Transformation of American Religion: How We Actually Live Our Faith* (Chicago: University of Chicago Press, 2004).

tional impact a particular brand of Christianity may have on the believer—has become commonplace. Product preference trumps both scriptural and pastoral authority, let alone any classic warrants of a traditional faith community. This experientialism is not very subtle; it also is pervasive. It is intricately intertwined with numerous extraneous and demographic factors that configure personal identity and private tastes: for examples, generational codes of dress, urban versus suburban lifestyles, musical interests, voting habits, and so on. In large measure it has had the same effect on many other religious groups besides Christianity who have been flattened, along with the general economic landscape, by the steamroller of globalization.

Islam is a pertinent illustration. As Roy has made us aware, the "new *ummah*" (community) has proved to be fertile turf for the spread of radical jihadism. The new jihadism is as much the product of new media, with its intense psychological impact, as it is of Muslims striving to rediscover who they are. The word "fundamentalism," trotted out to describe religious zealotry, is really a misnomer: it implies a scriptural literalism with no bearing whatsoever on the new politically turbocharged experientialism in religion. Fundamentalism was originally, at least in the early twentieth century, an epistemological rejection of the authority of modern science over the historic biblical worldview.

But Christian fundamentalism and jihadist Islam alike draw their energy from passionate moral and spiritual convictions inflamed by the postmodern fusion of electronic medium and message. The Western intelligentsia's familiar dismissal of these fundamentalisms as backward and ignorant reflects an equally ignorant and outdated bookish view regarding the sources of religious meaning and authority. In a not-so-nuanced sense these fundamentalisms are the cutting edge of globalized, and globalizing, religiosity.

Thrust into the futuristic urban and exurban planetscape through the nonlinear cognition and intensification of emotional focus that electronic media have spawned across cultures, these fundamentalisms have an enormous and authentic appeal, especially among the young. These very forces of globalization and deterritorialization have swiftly eroded local and parochial religious perspectives, like ocean breakers constantly crashing against fragile dunes. But at the same time through the explosion of new communications formats and networks, they have ironically and powerfully strengthened the absolutist and revelatory significance of ancient faith. Muhammad now "recites" the Qur'an right out in front of his cave to every emerging warrior prepared to take up the "sword of Islam." In "real time" Jesus "preaches" the Sermon on the Mount with electric guitars and a digital synthesizer rumbling behind him.

The radical relationality of the gospel summons has its own backup in the revelatory intensity of globo-electric communications processes. GloboChrist is no longer simply local. He is, as we have seen, glocal. Forget about the local church as the paradigm of Christian community. The principle of two or three gathering together still holds firm. But the gathering is simply the high-velocity acceleration of the force field of radical relationality. It ceases to be anchored merely in either the charismatic or structural authority of the religious leader, the preacher, or the board of elders. It emerges as a set of passionate one-on-one, or two-on-one, microresponses to the revelatory character of the Christian message in its complete kinesthetic setting and to its incarnation in the relational matrix of marriages, families, and friends.

Rhizomic. Gilles Deleuze's rhizome has come to be the perfect metaphor for the multiplication and interconnectivity of meaning in the postmodern moment. Its peculiar kind of rootedness belongs uniquely to the uprootedness—the deterritorialization—of postmodern culture and civilization. In that respect the rhizome is more radical than the radicalism of the modern era with its relentless "progress" and the mass movements and mobilizations of politics, labor, warfare, and communications that pulled people up from their roots and distinguished the modern era.

Deleuze's discovery of the rhizome as the root metaphor for a new theory of signs and meaning irrespective of its application to written languages is appropriate to the post-1960s development of global information systems and post-Einsteinian science. In his most important work, *A Thousand Plateaus*, Deleuze introduces the notion of the rhizome to counteract Western thought's fixed idea of reality as a book to be read. "The law of the book is the law of reflection," Deleuze writes, "the One that becomes two. How could the law of the book reside in nature, when it is what presides over the very division between world and book, nature and art? One becomes two; . . . what we have before us is the most classical and well-reflected, oldest, and weariest kind of thought. Nature doesn't work that way: in nature, roots are taproots with a more multiple,

lateral, and circular system of ramification, rather than a dichoto-
mous one. Thought lags behind nature."[4]

The book gives us binary or propositional logic, oppositional
politics, the subject-object distinction, and religious dualism. But
the natural form of the rhizome yields an entirely different way of
seeing and processing information that might be loosely characterized as "radically relational." The rhizome combines both "principles
of connection and heterogeneity." Any "point of a rhizome can be
connected to anything other, and must be." The Internet, or the
TCP-IP protocol on which it is based, has become the prevailing
postmodern model of information flow. The Internet is built on the
base, binary logic of the on-off switch in the silicon circuit.

Yet, almost paradoxically, as a communications system the Internet also apes Deleuze's rhizome. Technically, there is no such thing
as a "front end" and "back end" of the Internet. It has no center
and periphery. The Internet is not only decentered in the familiar
postmodern sense; the concept of centrality, privileged position,
height or depth also makes no sense whatsoever. "Unlike trees or
their roots, the rhizome connects any point to any other point, and
its traits are not necessarily linked to traits of the same nature; it
brings into play very different regimes of signs, and even nonsign
states."[5] A rhizome may be understood, according to Deleuze, as
the dynamic action of "multiplicities." A "multiplicity has neither
subject nor object, only determinations, magnitudes, and dimensions
that cannot increase in number without the multiplicity changing
in nature."[6]

While Deleuze's phraseology is challenging and not intuitively
easy, it is intended to suborn the human mind into glimpsing the
universe as movement and process, not as the accidental morphing of
fixed entities, a conceptual habit engrained in us by Western grammar itself. Western grammar demands that we conceive of things
in terms of substance and attributes, or subjects and predicates.
Rhizomes spread out and withdraw, split and segment, then re-form.
As Deleuze says, "You can never get rid of ants because they form
an animal rhizome that can rebound time and again after most of

4. Gilles Deleuze, *A Thousand Plateaus*, trans. Brian Massumi (Minneapolis:
University of Minnesota Press, 1987), 5.
5. Ibid., 21.
6. Ibid., 8.

it has been destroyed."[7] Similarly, the architecture of the Internet was originally defined by the United States Department of Defense to ensure unbreakable communication threads in times of nuclear explosions or other types of apocalyptic disaster. As a rhizome, the Internet goes everywhere because it does not need any right of way, as other communications and transportation networks require.

In the postmodern era of global interdependence and interlinkage, the growth of Christianity is surprisingly pursuing these unpredictable pathways of rhizomatic distribution, just as it did in the Roman Empire. Indigenization is one of the effects of the growth of rhizomes, since these "tubers without roots," as they have been called, send up different kinds of shoots wherever they happen to manifest. The rhizome goes where it grows, and grows where it goes.

A radical rhizomatic relationality that is revelatory of who God in Christ truly is—what Scripture calls Christ becoming "all in all"—gives us a broad theological inkling of what amounts to the body of Christ in the postmodern cosmopolis. Especially today, we should avoid immunizing ourselves against conceiving the immanent Christ in any other fashion than through Paul's familiar head, hands, and feet metaphor. As scholars have pointed out, "head-body" types of organizational theory were a hoary staple in Hellenistic social and political discourse long before Paul composed his Epistles. New Testament exegesis is making it more and more apparent that the language of early Christianity was dominated by the drive to relativize or deconstruct the brutal metaphysics of imperialism and emperor worship and to replace an immanent pagan politics with a transcendent theology of a Christ—the true Messiah and true Caesar—who reigned *because* he had conquered death by undergoing the horrifying and humiliating fate of crucifixion. Such an emperor could now be visualized as the genuine, though heavenly, head of an invisible cosmopolis that had been made immanent in a manner radically different from the Roman method—a ruthless subjugation of peoples by Roman legions and the exploitation of their natural wealth.

One prominent effort to apply Deleuze's philosophy to the emerging global situation appears in the work of Michael Hardt and Antonio Negri. Hardt and Negri, who write together in the way Deleuze and Guattari did in France a generation ago, have sought to

7. Ibid., 9.

cobble together what might be characterized as a theory of the global commons. Hardt and Negri distinguish their theory from political theory. It is the theory not of the *polis*—hence "politics"—but of the emergent organization and dynamics of the planetary *demos* in a borderless and largely stateless interweaving of populations and peoples in migration.

Some scholars have speculated that our current globopomo world, though marked by increasing prosperity rather than economic decline, strangely mimics that historical interlude between classical and medieval civilization that has at times been termed the "Dark Ages," the "age of migration," or the *Völkerwanderung* (German for "wandering of the peoples") that runs from about AD 500 to AD 1000. We are presently in another *Völkerwanderung*, when recognized national and social boundaries no longer seem to matter, and when the movement of peoples from site to site and place of employment to place of employment appears to go unchecked. The quaint notion of a civil society that has to be safeguarded by the political apparatus gives way to the haunting intuition that everything is up for grabs and that even though there remain formal statutes and conventions, they are rarely enforced for reasons of both impracticality and lack of consensus. Moreover, justice is built on the compulsion of needs rather than the majesty of the law. The debate over whether there actually should be anything that we might call "illegal immigration" echoes this deep tension and perplexity.

According to Hardt and Negri, this new *Völkerwanderung* calls for a brand-new geopolitics. "Geopolitics may regard borders as fixed but they are also . . . thresholds or points of passage." In addition, "the borders of geopolitics have to do with natural borders, conceived in either geographical, ethnic, or demographic terms. When geopolitics confronts borders posed as natural, in fact, it either uses them instrumentally or undermines them, setting in motion a slide toward expansion, going beyond."[8] Hardt and Negri, seeking to revive in politically palatable parlance the now-discredited doctrines of Karl Marx, regard the new global situation as the politics of empire advancing the interests of capital. To the kind of postindustrial and digital-age dynamics of globalization that Friedman celebrates, Hardt and Negri counterpose a new form of planetary

8. Michael Hardt and Antonio Negri, *Multitude: War and Democracy in the Age of Empire* (New York: Penguin, 2004), 314.

participatory democracy, which they describe as "the multitude against empire."

In *The Communist Manifesto*, Marx prophesied (wrongly) a transnational uprising of the oppressed industrial proletariat with "nothing to lose" but their "chains," once their "consciousness" is raised by the new, cosmopolitan intellectual elites and mobilized by the revolutionary vanguard. Hardt and Negri look to a similar refinement of the aspirations and dreams of what they regard as the amorphous postmodern global multitudes. Hardt and Negri envision a curious and indefinable sort of intelligent coagulation of the multitudes, which can include everyone in every land, from expropriated peasants to itinerant artists and political militants to laid-off knowledge workers after their high-paying jobs have been outsourced to South Asia.

Besting Marx, who anticipated a communist utopia—what Soviet propagandists cynically labeled a "workers' paradise"—Hardt and Negri await the rhizomic generation of somehow "cooperative apparatuses of production and community." They speak of an "inside" that serves as a kind of dike against the "outside" of what Austrian economist Joseph Schumpeter termed the "creative destruction" wrought by global capitalism. "This inside is the productive cooperation of mass intellectuality and affective networks, the productivity of postmodern biopolitics." The politics of the "inside" constitutes a "militancy" that "makes resistance into counterpower and makes rebellion into a project of love."

To underscore their point, Hardt and Negri invent the icon of a postmodern Francis of Assisi. "To denounce the poverty of multitude," they argue, Francis "adopted that common condition and discovered there the ontological power of a new society. . . . Francis in opposition to nascent capitalism refused every instrumental discipline, and in opposition to the mortification of the flesh . . . he posed a joyous life, including all of being and nature. . . . Once again in postmodernity we find ourselves in Francis's situation, posing against the misery of power the joy of being. This is a revolution that no power will control—because biopower and communism, cooperation and revolution remain together, in love, simplicity, and also innocence."[9]

---

9. Michael Hardt and Antonio Negri, *Empire* (Cambridge, MA: Harvard University Press, 2000), 413.

Here we have—in a true intellectual syncretism that spans the last thirty years from Che Guevara and the Beatles to contemporary eco-radicalism—an odd and intellectually disingenuous knockoff of Deleuze's authentic postmodern vision. After all is said and done, "all you need is love," da-ta-da-da-dun. Tertullian asked rather pointedly what Athens might have to do with Jerusalem; in this age of global upheaval, we seriously need to inquire of ourselves, and the leaders of the new emerging church chic need to listen closely: what does the next Christendom have really to do with a decadent and dying Western liberal-lite hippiedom? The answer—Tertullian's answer—is simple: Nothing! Nothing at all! Nada! *Rein nichts*!

Why not? Relationality is the radical opposite of what left-wing utopianism from Joachim of Fiore to Timothy Leary to Hardt and Negri have exalted as the spiritual alternative to power and domination: abstract human solidarity. Communitarianism, or something we might dub *solidarism*, the fetishism of the Western intellectual elites, constitutes the idolatry of the social will to power over God's will, power, and sovereignty. Using the philosopher G. W. F. Hegel's phrase, communitarianism—the acceptable, politically correct version of the orgy—is the ethical "night when all cows are black," the washing out of all real and concrete relational commitments. There can be no more democratic "multitudinism" in the era of global deterritorialization than there can be a work ethic at a convention of trust-funders.

In practice, multitudinism as a social ethic comes down to pure libertarianism, particularly various forms of sexual and instinctual antinomianism. It is the narcissism of the advanced industrial-political elites masquerading as a politics of liberation. It is the same kind of narcissism that afflicted the "me generation" during the 1970s and 1980s. "We-ness" turned out to be nothing other than a shill for "me-ness," a me-ness that shouts the rhetoric of emancipation. But under the guise of a revolutionary summons, the me-ness in practice amounts to self-promotion of the interests of an advanced and largely amoral urban esthetic, with no value for the developing South.

Increasingly, the developing South is turning to forms of what we might term a *transcendent moral collectivism* as opposed to the immanent liberal communitarianism that has dominated Western progressive discourses as old-style industrial socialism morphed into the so-called cultural Marxism of the 1960s and beyond. The rhizomes of global migration, commerce, cultural diffusion, and communication have been pathways for not just the nomadic deterritorialization of regional cultural formations. They have also been the subtle filaments for the reterritorialization of uncompromising monotheism, signaled in the same moral and militant revolt of the underclasses against the self-indulgent individualism of the global ruling elites that marked the underground spread of Christianity during the late Roman Empire. The same kind of revolt marked the uprising of the desert peoples against the decadent Byzantine heirs to the Caesars, as in the first century of Islamic expansion. In many ways we have turned the clock back and find ourselves in the first half of the first millennium all over again.

Globalization as a Two-Edged Sword

Globalization is a powerful two-edged blade. It both unites and fragments, frees and enslaves, calls us into the solitude of ourselves and the unity of the whole. The struggle between privatism and collectivism is an old one, and it has defined the concept of modernity, and to a large extent the modern world. Before the fall of Communism, the contest between individualism and collectivism was couched almost exclusively in political and economic terms. In other words, most of the battles fought were derived from sectarian conflicts within the Enlightenment tradition of political economy. As most historians of thought acknowledge, Marxism constitutes what might be called "the radical reformation" when it comes to the debates over the ideal human society, systems of governance, and the nature of "man" characterizing the *Aufklärung*. The post-Communist age has not been an unmixed blessing for what no longer appears to be simply a triumphal global capitalism. A reactionary storm is brewing fast, and it is clearly contained in the martial music of a resurgent Muslim faith.

Revolutionary Islam, or Islamism, offers something that a secularized, thoroughly libertarian, and intellectually fractionated post-Christian West has lost, and that decadent Anglo-Europa ignores at its own eternal peril. It offers an eschatology of radical change based on a transcendental call to global, collective transformation. The spirit of postmodern revolutionary Islam is most explicit and concentrated in Sayyid Qutb's *Ma'ālim fī al-tarīq* (*Milestones/*

Signposts along the Road/Way), published in 1964, shortly before
his death. Some refer to the book as the manifesto for contemporary revolutionary Islam. In it Qutb basically identifies the secular,
contemporary West as embodying the pagan pre-Islamic state of
jahiliyya, "ignorance." Just as the armies of Islam in the seventh
century mobilized to rid the world of *jahiliyya*, so today's Muslim
militants must take up the sword of Islam once again. The book
may have directly inspired the formation of al-Qaida through bin
Laden's Egyptian mentor Ayman al-Zawahiri, whose brother was
a key promoter of Qutb's ideas over two decades.

One of Qutb's immediate apostles and exegetes, M. A. Muqtedar
Khan, explains the matter as follows: "Qutb gives an interesting
twist to the idea of *jahiliyya*. *Jahiliyya* for Qutb is the sovereignty of
man over man [as in] socio-political orders where men have power
over other men, to institute legislation and determine principles
of right and wrong conduct. The Qur'an is explicit in postulating
Islam as the antithesis of *jahiliyya*. Qutb, by redefining *jahiliyya*
to encompass modern secular systems of political organization, is
basically decreeing that all existing systems are unacceptable and
even antithetical to the spirit of Islam."[10] Qutb writes: "Islam knows
only two kinds of societies, the Islamic and the *jahili*. The Islamic
society is that which follows Islam in belief and ways of worship, in
law and organization, in morals and manners. The jahili society is
that which does not follow Islam and in which neither the Islamic
belief and concepts, nor Islamic values or standards, Islamic laws
and regulations, or Islamic morals and manners are cared for."[11]

Qutb is arguing that only the radical unity (*tawhid*) of the faith
under one worldwide Islamic form of governance can solve the
problems, let alone the spiritual malaise, of what we now know as
postmodern humanity. Western differentialism and cultural heterogeneity must give way to both a moral and political monotheism,
an idea that inspired Khomeini and the 1979 Islamic Revolution in
Iran. "The Islamic civilization can take various forms in its material
and organizational structure, but the principles and values on which
it is based are eternal and unchangeable. These are: the worship of

10. M. A. Muqtedar Khan, "An Executive Summary" of *Milestones*, by Sayyid
Qutb, accessed December 14, 2006, http://www.youngmuslims.ca/online_library/books/
milestones/freshlook.asp.
11. Sayyid Qutb, *Milestones* (Cedar Rapids, IA: Mother Mosque Foundation,
1981), 93.

God alone, the foundation of human relationships on the belief in the Oneness of God, the supremacy of the humanity of man over material things, the development of human values and the control of animalistic desires, respect for the family, the assumption of being the representative of God on earth according to His guidance and instruction, and in all affairs of this vicegerency the rule of God's law (al-Shari'ah) and the way of life prescribed by Him."[12]

In other words, everything that has been associated with postmodern liberalism and libertarianism, with autonomy and freedom from what Immanuel Kant called "heteronomous" authority, everything that has compelled modern secularism and in large measure the postmodern response, can be boiled down to *jahiliyya*, which must be attacked, conquered, and subjugated. The unimaginably naive and mindless supposition of contemporary Western liberalism that revolutionary Islam has precipitated from nothing more than a kind of mass disgruntlement with capitalist exploitation, American militarism, or a general social inequality that can somehow be remedied by pacifist and economically redistributionist policies that are still based on some form of secular political immanentism has blinded us to the real forces behind the gathering storm.

Two critical factors to Islam rising have to be brought out into the open. One, as we have already suggested, is the long cultural memory of the Middle East and its grievances against the West for having invaded its space in the first place—not, as is commonly assumed, for its past colonialist sins. With the exception of the 1920s and early 1930s (when following the First World War Britain and France dominated the region essentially as occupying powers), true Western colonialism—especially in comparison with how it was manifested in Africa and Asia—never established a hegemony in the Middle East. From World War I onward, Western oil interests tried to operate as quasi-colonial protectorates, but at first they were repeatedly thwarted by local governments, later by Soviet foreign policy, and eventually by pan-Arabic and pan-Islamic movements.

The other factor is the unifying appeal of Islam itself. Qutb was prescient in the 1950s and 1960s, when he realized that no matter what the West did or how Muslim peoples sought to adopt Western attitudes and mores, the call of the minaret would never fade from Middle Eastern consciousness. In fact, once the Muslim nations

12. Ibid., 104.

became disenchanted in their coy flirtation with Western secularism, he understood, they would embrace his uncompromising message as they had embraced Muhammad centuries earlier. He was right. Islam has a history of explosive outbreaks—we are witnessing one now—because of its world vision and its jihadist alternative to the Great Commission, which has been a powerful incentive for Muslims confronted with the military might of the "Christian" West. The current dynamic has nothing to do with any anticolonial—or in current parlance, "antiglobalist"—countercrusade. It has nothing to do with the cheap socialist romanticism of the American and European left, of which Qutb is quite contemptuous.[13] Qutb ironically agrees with Samuel Huntington that we are witnessing a clash of civilizations, but in his view it is a clash (a jihad) of the "superior" one (Islamic) against the decadent and inferior one (the West).

In *Milestones*, Qutb calls Islam "the real civilization." He affirms Islamic civilization with the same moralistic and in no sense ironic fervor as Kipling asserted the superiority of Western Christendom when he spoke of "the white man's burden." Just as Christendom through colonial aggression battled ignorance and savagery, according to Kipling, the resurgent Muslim "empire" through jihad must battle *jahiliyya*, the most flagrant example of which is the secular materialism and consumerism of the West. Qutb called for "vast and far-reaching" changes throughout the world, inspiring perhaps al-Qaida's decision to assault the West on the West's own doorstep.

These changes will come only through revolutionary violence, Qutb suggests. Suicide bombings, plane hijackings, and attacks on civilians were not concrete strategies that Qutb necessarily pictured, but they are consistent with "the call" he issued. The call is to jihad until the "vast and far-reaching" changes are realized. The "road" of which his book was the first "signpost" or "milestone" is the profound and protracted struggle to which the West with its increasingly Disneylandish war on terror is almost clueless in its response. Qutb concludes his manifesto with a chilling convocation. This "intricate point" of *Milestones*, Qutb writes,

13. "The struggle between the Believers and their enemies is in essence a struggle of belief, and not in any way of anything else. The enemies are angered only because of their faith, enraged only because of their belief. This was not a political or an economic or a racial struggle; had it been any of these, its settlement would have been easy, the solution of its difficulties would have been simple. But essentially it was a struggle between beliefs—either unbelief or faith, either Jahiliyyah or Islam" (ibid., 159).

requires deep thought by all callers toward God, to whatever country
or period of time they belong; for this guarantees that they will be
able to see the milestones of the road clearly and without ambiguity,
and establishes the path for those who wish to traverse it to the end,
whatever this end may be; then what God intends to do with His
Call and with them is up to Him. Then they will not be anxious,
while traversing this road ever paved with skulls and limbs and blood
and sweat, to find help and victory, or desirous that the decision
between the truth and falsehood be made on this earth. However,
if God Himself intends to fulfill the completion of His call and His
religion through their efforts, He will bring about His will—but not
as a reward for their sufferings and sacrifices. Indeed, this world is
not a place of reward.[14]

Christianity's Transcendental Call

But Christianity has an even more powerful transcendental call.
Unlike Islam, however, the call is both immanent and transcendent
at the same time. The four-dimensionality of Christ's cross moves
us in that direction. The call of the GloboChrist is indigenizing and
incarnational. What does that mean in nontechnical, nontheological
parlance? Secular liberalism, if there really is such a phenomenon
that we can easily discern and trace through modern history, has
since at least the seventeenth century borne the global trend of
what Deleuze terms "pure immanence." The trend culminated in
the latter part of the twentieth century and was expressed in the
death-of-God movement of the 1960s, which has lately resurfaced
in a curious retroguise that calls itself "secular theology." The pure
immanence of secular theology has its counterfoil in Qutbian-style
radical Islamism, and it is no accident that the latter identifies the
spirit of the age embodied in the former as the essence of *jahiliyya*,
against which relentless jihad must be waged.

The kind of radical, relational, and incarnational Christian witness that a postmodernized Great Commission entails would have
the ferocity of the jihad and paradoxically also the love for the lost
that Jesus demonstrated. Unfortunately, the postmodern West has
been deeply afflicted by a passivity and a privatized sentimentality
that makes the passion of commitment to God's dramatic future

14. Ibid., 158.

virtually impossible. It is not a question of moral relativity versus the sovereignty of absolutes, on which evangelical theology almost pathologically continues to dwell. The challenge of postmodernity has nothing to do with the old Reformation issue of authority. All forms of authority have collapsed in the West, even among so-called fundamentalists, who comprise the membership rolls of "Bible churches." Even among those who constantly cry "Lord, Lord," it is not Christ, but the consumerist ethic of personal satisfaction—the lubricant of Deleuze's "desiring machines"—that has been installed idolatrously in the holy of holies. Post-Christendom has met its own abomination of desolation in an all-pervasive metaphysics of self that must wither and rapidly burst into flames before the advancing phalanx of fire we know as militant Islam.

The relational imperative is not conditional. It is categorical, as the philosopher Immanuel Kant would say. Thus as Christians we have no option but to submit to it. Jesus commanded that we make disciples—not religious consumers—of all nations. Discipling demands discipline, as the etymology of the term implies. But even more important, discipling requires a singular focus on relationships, relationships that incarnate the pure love of God for his fallen creatures, as shown at Calvary.

The proof text for this insight is John 13:34 and following. The context is Jesus's Last Supper, when he intimates what will soon be occurring, that he will be arrested and finally executed. He tells his disciples, whom he had chosen, that he is going to a place where "you cannot come." In other words, he is going to the cross. Peter proudly says that he will "lay down" his life for his master, but Jesus rebukes him and informs him that he will be cowed by the crisis he is about to face and will deny his master. Jesus goes on to say that Peter will eventually "follow" him, but in a somewhat oblique manner, often missed by Christian exegetes, he is proposing that what Dietrich Bonhoeffer called "the cost of discipleship" is too high at the moment for even his own followers. The cost of discipleship is not necessarily "giving up one's life," as Jesus was prepared to do. Jesus is not issuing a call to martyrdom so much as uncompromising commitment to one another in love. That is what discipleship truly signifies. "I give you a new commandment, that you love one another. Just as I have loved you, so you should love one another. By this everyone will know that you are my disciples, if you have love for one another" (John 13:34–35 NRSV).

Jesus's use of the phrasing "a new commandment" is frequently scanted in light of its implicit ramifications. Because Jesus at the Last Supper has executed the "new covenant" with his disciples, the Great Commandment itself now acquires an unprecedented meaning. Its new meaning belongs to this sudden revelation not merely about who God is but also about what love is. Previously the Great Commandment bade us to love God and our neighbor. Now this love can be comprehended only in an incarnational situation. Its incarnate presence is the activation of profound rhizomic relations that explode from the center toward the ends of the earth. We are commanded to be incarnational in relation to one another just as God at the cross was incarnational in Christ.

Discipleship is no longer linear but radial. As God now is "in Christ" in the pure "Emmanuel" modality, as God with us, thus in our love for one another as true disciples we are manifesting the radical, rhizomic, relational, and revelatory power of Christ himself. We are no longer simply Christ's "followers"—the pre-Easter form of relation to a master-and-teacher that is conventionally called "disciple"—but also perpetual Christ incarnators ("disciples" in the post-Easter and perhaps—dare we say?—powerful postmodern sense of the term). We are Christs to one another! We are harbingers of the eschaton, when Christ through us will become "all in all."

6

And Then the End Will Come

> Christ beside me, Christ before me, Christ behind me, Christ within me, Christ beneath me, Christ above me.
>
> The prayer of Saint Patrick

Eschatology Redux

Eschatology has not been a fashionable mode of discourse in contemporary Christian literature. Pop eschatology, however, has been much in vogue in recent years, but it has been an almost exclusive preoccupation of premillennial dispensational fundamentalism, as the staggering book sales of the Left Behind series attest. The Islamic world's version of pop eschatology, centered on the mystique of a heroic end-times military figure called the Mahdi, has also been gaining momentum, particularly in Iran. Mahdism has been a significant component of Shiite Islam for centuries, and there is strong evidence that the Iranian leadership that came to power in 2005 was more directly influenced by this strand of thinking than any cleric since the Iranian Islamic Revolution of 1979. Sociologists of religion routinely explain a rise in eschatological expectations as the outgrowth of irresolvable social tensions, in this case stemming from the stresses of economic globalization.

Yet the anticipation of the end not only is deeply rooted in Scripture but also was the fervent hope of the early Christian church. In a manner that modern and postmodern theologians have regularly failed to grasp, such hope has at the same time been the pivotal theological image of thought for Christianity as a whole, insofar as it defines the ultimate historical hope and the incomparable meaning of the Easter event (cf. 1 Cor. 15:20–28). There can be no ecclesiology without eschatology, and vice versa.

In Western religious liberalism and to a large extent even in what has come to be termed Christian postmodernism, the doctrines and formulations that can be regarded as eschatological have been given short shrift and often treated with derision. Popular eschatological best sellers in America, from Hal Lindsay's *The Late Great Planet Earth* (1970) to the more recent Left Behind series authored by Tim LaHaye and Jerry Jenkins, have fueled this attitude. Such books, which have sold millions of copies over the years, represent a fanciful and melodramatic take on the end-times theology of nineteenth-century evangelist Charles Darby, which came to be known as premillennial dispensationalism. Increasingly, anyone who takes Christian eschatology seriously is lumped in with fundamentalists. But this linkage amounts to guilt by association and gives a misleading picture of Christian eschatology as a whole.

The word *eschatology* derives from the Greek *eschatos*, meaning "end." Throughout Christian history the theme of the eschaton has been remarkably persistent and has remained a subject not only for lavish and lurid interpretations but also for ferocious quarrels. Essentially, all discussions regarding eschatology range over three key areas of concern: the parousia, or second coming, of Jesus; the nature of the afterworld and the new order of things that is supposed to follow the climax of time and history; and the signs of the end and the sequence of events leading up to it.

During the first century, the focus for the most part fell on what many believed to be Jesus's own imminent return. Jesus's departure from this world after the resurrection, most early Christians assumed, would result in his absence for only a short time. When a century or so elapsed, the early church had to contend with what scholars have dubbed the "delay of the parousia." At that time the character of Christianity itself—not just its eschatology—significantly changed. The church began to organize as a permanent religious institution and to incorporate the patterns of administration unique to Roman imperial society. What we now call the "Catholic" church had its beginnings during this period of both disillusionment and redirection.

Rome's brutal quashing of a revolt by the inhabitants of Judea in AD 70 led to the destruction of the temple at Jerusalem and the expulsion of Jews from Jerusalem. The event, foretold by Jesus, also had a profound effect on the formation of early Christianity. Before that time most Christians were either Judean Jews or Jews of the Mediterranean Diaspora, or Dispersion. After the destruction of the temple, Christianity became increasingly a gentile faith and began to draw the suspicions of Roman magistrates throughout the empire, who sometimes confused it with Judaism. Once it had become predominantly gentile, the church was less concerned with Christ's return than it was with the destiny of the human soul upon physical death.

This change was the result of two factors. First, Jesus had claimed to be Israel's Messiah, and he promised to return in glory to rule as such. His messianic kingdom, however, would not be confined just to Judea. It would encompass "all the nations." The early Christian messianic expectation was based on the exalted universalism of the prophecies of Second Isaiah (Isa. 44–55), which most scholars trace to the sixth century BC. Yet when Judea was wrecked by the Romans, the older messianic anticipation lost its cogency and credibility. Furthermore, for the new gentile Christians who increasingly comprised the church, the idea of Jesus as an enthroned king of Israel was quite unintelligible and certainly not very compelling.

In trying to reconcile the actual messianic language of the Gospels and Paul's Letters with what actually occurred during the first century, contemporary scholars known as preterists (from the Greek prefix signifying what is "past") have begun to give explanations of baffling prophecies from the New Testament as once "future" events that have now been fulfilled. In recent years preterism has been gaining adherents among conservative evangelical thinkers who have been disgusted or embarrassed by the absurdities of so much premillennial dispensationalism. One prominent preterist position is that Christ actually returned when the temple at Jerusalem was razed. The view is adduced from a reading of Matthew 24—the so-called Little Apocalypse of the New Testament—where Jesus talks about the "end" distinctly in reference to the destruction of the temple.[1]

Second, the early church altered its end-times message after the failed revolt because the very meaning of faith now had radically distinct connotations for its overwhelmingly gentile audience. By this time Mediterranean paganism had centered on mystery religions or personal cults of salvation. These cults aimed to guarantee the devotee a direct experience of the god, or goddess, which supposedly guaranteed "salvation." Each of these deities was commonly known as a savior, or *sōtēr*. Salvation was no longer future, but immediate. The early church, therefore, adopted Jewish language of the imminent end times to the new situation. Eschatology became soteriology. Salvation was personal, though it was now deferred to a future life, what rabbinic Judaism began to term the "world to come."

Old-style eschatology, comparable to what is found in the book of Revelation, certainly continued to captivate the imaginations of the faithful. From time to time the early church would be shaken by unexpected millennial fervor; end-time prophets who called into question the beliefs and practices of the orthodox establishment would appear unexpectedly. The most notable of these millennial outbursts was the movement in the second century known as Montanism, which attracted even such a sober orthodox church father as Tertullian. Like many radical sects that would discomfit the church hierarchy for generations, the Montanists, who elevated the role of women and are sometimes tagged as forerunners of modern Pentecostalism, had little good to say about a church that had made its peace, or attempted to make its peace, with the world. After throwing in his lot with the Montanists, Tertullian began contemptuously referring to the Christian establishment as the "church of all those bishops."

As Norman Cohn continues to remind us, eschatology will not go away. In his classic work *The Pursuit of the Millennium: Revolutionary Millenarianism and Mystical Anarchists of the Middle Ages*, Cohn describes the way in which the ancient eschatologies

1. "Jesus left the temple and was walking away when his disciples came up to him to call his attention to its buildings. 'Do you see all these things?' he asked. 'I tell you the truth, not one stone here will be left on another; every one will be thrown down.' As Jesus was sitting on the Mount of Olives, the disciples came to him privately. 'Tell us,' they said, 'when will this happen, and what will be the sign of your coming and of the end of the age?'" (Matt. 24:1–3).

continued to inflame the imagination of the socially and culturally disaffected for centuries after the fall of Rome and up into the modern era.[2] Starting with the turn of the first millennium, wandering prophets and evangelists warned Christendom that the conclusion of all things was at hand. The coming Manichaean battle between good and evil was preached in the streets from Paris to Cologne, and it was construed in political as well as theological terms.

Meanwhile, Europe was wracked with religious and sectarian uprisings. Crusades were urged, and Jews were routinely massacred. By the sixteenth century, millenarianism had fed popular discontent with such fervor that the expectation of Christ's impending return triggered widespread and violent uprisings among the underclasses. The most telling of these revolts was the Peasants' War in Germany from 1524 to 1525. The Peasants' War was driven by deep rage toward the system of oppressive taxation associated with the transition from feudalism to the monarchial state in the late Middle Ages. But it was expressed in end-of-the-world rhetoric. Millenarian fervor spread all across Europe and was championed by such charismatic leaders as Thomas Müntzer and John of Leiden. These figures resembled twentieth-century Marxist revolutionaries and guerilla fighters. Indeed, Karl Marx's sidekick, Friedrich Engels, wrote an entire book about the Peasants' War in Germany and regarded it as the first genuine manifestation of revolutionary "class consciousness" in the Western world.

Messianism and Globalization

Scholars who have examined millenarian and eschatological excitement throughout history typically identify the phenomenon with the kinds of massive disruption of the existing social order that underlie social revolution. It is not surprising that the social and cultural stresses accompanying globalization have also generated, and are continuing to generate, a new eschatological outlook in many quarters. Yet whereas in the past millenarian outbreaks were confined largely to Christendom, they can be found today among

2. Norman Cohn, *The Pursuit of the Millennium: Revolutionary Millenarianism and Mystical Anarchists of the Middle Ages* (New York: Oxford University Press, 1970).

all the civilizations and are reaching a confluence as the new world disorder.

Eschatological vision and thinking are increasingly having an impact on international relations. For example, nineteenth-century Western millenarianism propelled not only a sense of "manifest destiny" for the new American republic but also the romantic nationalism behind the rise of fascist movements as well as the drive to return the Jews to Palestine; now it is clashing with a new apocalypticism affecting the Islamic world. The clash of civilizations is beginning to look like a war of eschatologies. The current conflict between Iran and the West stems from this particular dynamic.

For instance, according to an article in the *Christian Science Monitor*, an organization in Iran known as the Bright Future News Agency has created a national "messiah hotline" in an effort to motivate and mobilize the millions who believe in the "imminent return of the Mahdi," a Shiite figure whose coming is comparable to the second advent in Christianity. Indeed, many Shiites believe that when the Mahdi comes, he will be accompanied by Jesus, who will play a supporting role. According to Shiite lore, the Mahdi's return will be the start of a planetary battle between Islam and the forces of opposition. Islam will certainly win, and the world will see the triumph of the Muslim faith, and of Shiite Muslims in particular. The leading sect in Iran, known as the Twelver Shiite sect, maintains that "Imam Mahdi" will be none other than Muhammad ibn Hasan, who disappeared—or as Twelvers say, went into "occultation"—in the ninth century when he was only five years old.

The *Monitor* article tells a gripping tale of how Mahdist millennial fervor has consumed the average Iranian.

> While he waits, Morteza Rabaninejad sits at a new computer with a new telephone and a new headset, answering five calls and 10 letters a day. "Would you please explain all the signs of rising?" writes one correspondent. "What are the things we must do to make the Mahdi rise earlier than he is supposed to?" Started in 2004, the institute is the eighth of its kind in Iran to study and even speed the Mahdi's return. But it is the largest and most influential, with 160 staff, a growing reach in local schools, children's and teen magazines, and unlimited ambition to spread the word.[3]

3. See http://www.csmonitor.com/2006/0104/p07s02-wome.html.

Iran's radical and confrontational president Mahmoud Ahmadinejad has been instrumental in whipping up this fever. Ahmadinejad's speech to the United Nations in 2006 was topped off with an apocalyptic flourish that left most secular and political commentators on world affairs scratching their heads. Ahmadinejad called on Allah to hasten the emergence of the Mahdi on the world scene.

Muslims must be prepared to take control of the affairs of the entire world. According to a report that appeared in some Western newspapers in the early part of 2006, Ahmadinejad proclaimed to an enormous gathering of theological students in Qom, Iran's holy city: "We must believe in the fact that Islam is not confined to geographical borders, ethnic groups, and nations. It's a universal ideology that leads the world to justice."[4]

Iraqi intelligence sources translated the text of the speech and communicated it to Western leaders. The triumph of the Islamic revolution until Ayatollah Ruhollah Khomeini in 1979 had rekindled Mahdist fervor, which has always lurked under the surface and has broken out at unexpected times in the history of Shiite Islam. Although Khomeini did not countenance the implication that he was in fact the long awaited Mahdi, or "hidden imam," he did not actively discourage it either. As it turned out, Khomeini cleverly transformed the desire for the appearance of the Mahdi into a quasi-Western ideology of immanent revolution and orchestrated what some scholars have termed "activist Mahdism," entailing the imposition of Islamic law, or Sharia, on society and spreading revolution wherever it is feasible in order to prepare the way for the appearance of the hidden imam.

Despite Western woolgathering, this strategy has been in place for almost three decades in Iran. Ahmadinejad's extremism calls for the destruction not just of Israel but also of the Western powers, and does not seem to be some kind of errant anomaly but represents the culmination of a messianic politics that has deep roots in both Iranian history and discernible strands of Islam itself. Not only has Ahmadinejad heavily funded Mahdist speculation and activism among students and clerics in present-day Iran; numerous conferences have also been held and books released to fuel the excitement. If we can believe certain statements by Iranian clerics, most of which

4. "Iran's Ahmadinejad: Sharon dead and 'others to follow suit,'" *Iran Focus,* January 5, 2006, http://www.iranfocus.com/modules/news/article.php?storyid=5166.

have never been translated out of Farsi, almost half a million books focusing on the Mahdi were printed in Qom in 2005.

Iranian Islamic millenarianism is centered on *mahdaviat*, a term employed in certain forms of Shiism. It refers to a belief in, as well as active preparation for, the impending return of the Mahdi. Ahmadinejad has been rumored to have predicted the return before the end of 2007. He is also said to have had his aides drop a list of his cronies down a well from which the Madhi is supposed to emerge and lead the battle on that decisive day. According to the report, the list contains the names of Ahmadinejad's recommendations to the Mahdi for his divine cabinet, once the latter's reign of "peace and justice" is inaugurated. This strange behavior can be explained by Mahdist doctrine and folklore down through the ages. Just as in the Christian tradition Jesus ascended into heaven on the promise that he would be coming back "on the clouds," so in this version of Islam the Mahdi went into "occultation" (*ghaybat*), or hiding, and is getting ready to reveal himself once the time is ripe.

The doctrine of occultation is closely tied in with the Shiite practice of *taqiyya*, or "dissemblance/deception/concealment." The dissolution of the Abbasid Empire in the Middle East at the end of the ninth century AD, notes Abdulaziz Sachedina, led to brutal suppression of the Shiites and forced them and their imams into hiding. "The Imams had encouraged the employment of *taqiyya* and had declared it to be an incumbent act on their followers."[5] The emphasis on invisibility and deception as strategic ploys for facilitating world-shaking change and revolution, of the kind witnessed in Iran when Khomeini came to power in the late 1970s, obviously has serious implications for understanding the nature of both the political and religious strife presently engulfing the planet.

But it is not a matter of politics on the one hand and religious otherworldliness on the other hand, as the Western dualist mind-set is apt to frame the problem. According to Kaveh Afrasiabi, "The occultation and divine hope in the end of history are two sides of the same eschatological event. They point back to the promises of final reappearance of the savior that can only be understood as the

5. Abdulaziz A. Sachedina, *Islamic Messianism: The Idea of the Mahdī in Twelver Shī'ism* (Albany: New York State University Press, 1981), 29.

continuation of God's self-manifestation and self-involving nature in the relation with the world, especially with humanity."[6]

In other words, the hidden savior is the key to the final days when the world will be turned upside down and disorder will give way to divine order. The Mahdist script is not all that different from the New Testament prophecy of the sudden and surprising revealing of the heavenly Messiah, or Son of Man. Jesus prophesied:

> For then there will be great distress, unequaled from the beginning of the world until now—and never to be equaled again. If those days had not been cut short, no one would survive, but for the sake of the elect those days will be shortened. At that time if anyone says to you, "Look, here is the Christ!" or, "There he is!" do not believe it. For false Christs and false prophets will appear and perform great signs and miracles to deceive even the elect—if that were possible. See, I have told you ahead of time. So if anyone tells you, "There he is, out in the desert," do not go out; or, "Here he is, in the inner rooms," do not believe it. For as lightning that comes from the east is visible even in the west, so will be the coming of the Son of Man. (Matt. 24:21–27)

In the Christian scenario the stressful days preceding the end will be marked by moral confusion and earthly conflict of a magnitude never encountered in the past. In the Islamic perspective, things will be quite similar. "Sin, in the form of fornication, drunkenness, great inequalities in wealth, women in positions of authority, everything just short of dogs and cats living openly together, will increase. . . . Colossal earthquakes will strike, and great smoke will issue from Yemen."[7] At this point a complicated pageant of heroes and villains, which is slightly different from the more simplified scenario in Christian tradition, occupies the historical stage. These figures include the Dajjal, "the Deceiver" (the Islamic equivalent of the "antichrist"); al-Dabbah, "the beast"; the mysterious *Yajuj wa-Majuj* (a transliteration of the biblical Gog and Magog); *al-Sufyani* (a somewhat nebulous personage who may be a caricature of an "evil" caliph in early Muslim times); and Jesus.

    6. Kaveh L. Afrasiabi, "Shiism Mahdism: Reflections on a Doctrine of Hope," http://www.payvand.com/news/03/nov/1126.html.
    7. Timothy R. Furnish, *Holiest Wars: Islamic Mahdis, Their Jihads, and Osama bin Laden* (Westport, CT: Praeger, 2005).

In some Muslim eschatological scripts, Jesus is not, as one might surmise, a bit player. He is more important than Muhammad himself, who happened simply to be a messenger while on earth. Jesus is at least commensurate with the Mahdi in stature. When he "returns," so far as these accounts are concerned, Jesus is a fully committed Muslim, whose mission is to make real and explicit what Muhammad's Qur'an predicted, as opposed to the teachings of Jesus the Jew. Since Muslims of all stripes maintain that the Qur'an perfects the teachings of the Jews and Christians, the "People of the Book," while rectifying the great errors (e.g., Jesus's death and resurrection) contained in Christian doctrine, it is only natural that Islamic eschatology of necessity includes a starring role for Jesus.

But the superficial similarities are dwarfed by monumental differences, a point that so many well-motivated efforts to find common ground among the Abrahamic religions blindly overlook. Eschatology and soteriology are intimately embraced with each other. In the history of religions, end-times pageants are little more than theatrical enactments of the more-subtle dramas in which the founders of the faith as human protagonists were caught up. Eschatology, therefore, is the ultimate, cosmic confirmation—what Muslims through the Qur'an and Christians through the book of Revelation would call unsealing, or opening the seals—of the truth that was not yet realized during the founders' lifetimes. Even Buddhism, though rigorously antihistorical in its orientation, developed a kind of distinctive eschatology after it was transplanted to the Far East.

A Collision of Eschatologies

The globopomo resurgence of religion has set us on an inescapable collision of eschatologies. As we have seen, this collision ultimately arises out of the profound presence of nonnegotiable differences at the soteriological core of each faith. From a theological standpoint, eschatology is not simply the ultimate disclosure of the truth of God. It is also the supernova-like revelation of difference in the sense of a grand separation of the truth from the lie, which in Christianity is conveyed through animal husbandry (e.g., sheeps and goats) and agricultural (e.g., the harvest) kinds of metaphors. If there is any one thing that renders postmodern philosophy—particularly the work of Derrida and Deleuze—highly consequential in this critical age, it is the fact that such thought, as opposed to modern and classical thought—hones in on the meaning and power of difference.

A liberal Christian, or even post-Christian, global civil society that allows a loose and mutually respectful—if not tolerant—recital of differences is looming as increasingly less possible in our globo-pomo environment. Jacques Derrida and Gianni Vattimo—the two chief protagonists of the colloquium on the island of Capri that, at least in Europe, inaugurated the new postmodern philosophical conversations on the meaning of faith—have pointed us in some-what different directions. Derrida cannot annul or even weaken the power of difference in his reflections on the significance of what he calls "faith and knowledge." In many respects the Capri discussions represent a somewhat self-tortured undertaking on Derrida's part to find a filament of coherence within his ongoing push for a uni-versal, radical style of what an earlier generation would have called "participatory democracy," which encourages the play of different views and interpretations.

The temptation for anyone recognizing the reality of pluralism while promoting the pursuit of difference, however, is to let oneself slide down the slick slope of incaution into the icy waters of moral and spiritual relativism. How can one remain faithful to the one, almighty God who demands our undivided allegiance and attention in a postmodern world where options and possibilities are forever multiplying, where different discourses about what is divine and holy continue to proliferate, where easy ethical formulas and models of personal integrity dissolve day by day into convoluted dilemmas and hard choices, for which no simple set of Christian maxims or a simple algorithm for everyday decision making becomes obvious?

The case of Dietrich Bonhoeffer has always been instructive for us. Bonhoeffer has been something of an enigma for today's new evangelical Christians. Widely read and renowned in America as the forerunner of secular theology by mainline Protestants during the late 1950s and the 1960s, his celebrity status drooped during the next two decades, only to be rediscovered by young evangelicals in the 1990s. Most of the interest in Bonhoeffer during the early period was prompted by the themes and controlling ideas of one particular book, his *Letters and Papers from Prison*. The book was composed during the last years of World War II, when Bonhoeffer was incar-cerated and eventually executed by the Nazis not only for aiding the escape of Jews but also for his involvement in the well-documented plot to assassinate Hitler.[8]

The *Letters and Papers* contrast unmistakably with the tone and thought of his previous works, which were grounded in both neo-orthodoxy and the kind of existential theology that prevailed in Europe between the wars. They are journal entries, much more personal and far more radical than anything he had authored before. They also reflect a sense of struggle with the more comforting and classical nostrums of theology, a struggle precipitated by the horrors of life under the Nazi regime at the end of the war, the same struggle experienced by Jews who lived through and later reflected back on the Holocaust. In the *Letters and Papers*, Bonhoeffer issued what twenty years later became catchphrases of the death-of-God movement—"man come of age" and "religionless Christianity"—that appealed to late 1960s radical Protestants, most of whom were also social activists. But some leading postmodern evangelicals of the 1990s rediscovered the more substantial and systematic work of the Bonhoeffer of the late 1920s and 1930s, when he was a university teacher and leader of the Confessing Church, which opposed the rise of fascism, ultimately reshaped evangelical theology, and made it less individualistic and more community oriented.

Bonhoeffer's theological writings cannot be divorced from the gripping historical drama in which his own personal life was immersed. From the start his antifascist activism snowballed until he came to a point where he realized that the enormity of evil concentrated in the Third Reich called for an unprecedented response and a searching of the Christian conscience in ways that probably few Christians had ever faced. Bonhoeffer, like many historians of the period, realized that Hitler was able to push ahead with his monstrous mission because of the passivity of Europe's Christians, not only in Germany but also in the occupied countries. Paul's injunction in Romans 13 to obey the "governing authorities" because they are instituted by God had been a matter of conscience equally for Christians, both Catholic and Protestant, and tragically it played into the hands of the Nazi propagandists.

When Bonhoeffer was offered an opportunity to assist in the plot against Hitler, it caused great consternation and internal conflict,

8. See Dietrich Bonhoeffer, *Letters and Papers from Prison* (London: SCM, 2001).

perhaps similar to Luther the night before he would appear before the Diet of Worms in 1521 and give his famous *"Hier stehe ich"* (Here I stand) statement. Luther had anguished over the question of how he, a lone monk, could be right and how over a thousand years of church teaching and authority could turn out to be wrong. Bonhoeffer knew that it was absolutely wrong and unconscionable for a Christian to become involved in a murder plot, particularly of a God-ordained ruler like the Führer. But somehow he discovered deep within his spirit that he had to do it, in part because he had the political connections to help the plot succeed. He knew that he could not stand idly by and acquiesce, as did most of his country-men, to the mass extermination of the Jews that was going on all around him, which weighed heavily on his conscience and would have continued to do so even more.

In an almost paradoxical sense, Bonhoeffer made a moral choice that could be considered relativistic but arose out of a profound faithfulness and commitment to the injunction and will of God. He knew that God wanted him to go against all the dictates of religion. Because they were merely obiter dicta, we do not know what Bonhoeffer ultimately meant by a "religionless Christianity." But, contrary to the cultural triumphalism of the secular theologians of the 1960s, it seems evident that Bonhoeffer was not in some fatu-ous manner celebrating the inherently Christian character of the dawning postmodern epoch. He certainly was not making a pitch for moral relativism, because he knew he was going against God's own ordinances for the sake of God, a God who could not at all be contained any longer in the old wineskins of Christian ethics. Bon-hoeffer knew that history itself had come to an apocalyptic pass and that something novel was coming forth, a tempestuous and confusing time when religion would go into eclipse while God would appear in a guise in which he had never shown himself before.

That characterization also certainly applies to the appearance of Jesus in Galilee in the first century. In certain important respects, Bon-hoeffer's thought, which was always grounded in the neo-orthodox premise of the Bible as God's unalloyed self-revelation to his crea-tures, led him in the duress of his last days on earth to a stuttering enunciation of what we are calling incarnational Christianity. His religionless Christianity was about going beyond the incarnation as a dogma that all Christians are obliged to confess at a propositional or conceptual level. It was about manifesting in our own lives Jesus, the Christ, as who he really was and who he said he was, as the living presence of God in the flesh.

Bonhoeffer was calling each of us through our own lives—what some have termed the life of the "martyr" (which in Greek means "witness")—to disclose that living presence in the most profound and challenging way at the extremities of human life itself. Incarnation is not just a once-in-a-human-lifetime sort of event. Jesus Christ was the firstfruits; now we are the complete harvest. Incarnation is the parousia, the fullness of the presence of God in that human flesh that defines itself as "sons and daughters" of the living God, as flesh of his flesh, as true Christians who are "of" and "belong to" Christ, who are Christ and little Christs to one another. "And I heard a loud voice from the throne saying, 'See, the home of God is among mortals, and he will dwell with them as their God'" (Rev. 21:3 NRSV). He will be Emmanuel in the most far-reaching meaning of the word, the God who is with us and who is always with us.

God dwelling with us and through us is what, theologically speaking, represents both the soteriological marker and the eschatological hope of the new globalized Christianity, the next Christendom. But the End will not come without the kind of final battle enshrined in the eschatological symbolism surrounding the word "Armageddon." It is not our plan or purpose here to find actual historical correlates, whether past, present, or future, for a literal Ἁρμαγεδδών, which in Greek (Rev. 16:16) most likely mimicks the Hebrew *Har Meggido* (Hill/Mount of Megiddo), referring to the site in Judea where many crucial battles were fought in ancient times. But the luxuriant lore of Armageddon in eschatology points us toward a truth to which all irenic styles of social gospel or Christian political progressivism fatefully blind us, or biblical fundamentalism trivializes out of its obsession with using its own intellectual GPS to pinpoint the date, time, and precise turn of events for the fulfillment of prophecy.

The truth we have in mind is the one Christ drove home to his disciples—that the triumph of the faith itself requires the "good fight," and a fight to the finish. As globalized Christianity surges forward, it is confronted with a countereschatology that has its own compelling history and tradition behind it. We are referring to the eschatology inherent in the tradition inaugurated by the one whom his followers call the Prophet. The immediate future will be determined on a world scale by this clash of eschatologies, and there really is no room to reconcile them, if finding common ground among different revelations is what God ever had in mind. The challenge to the postmodern Christian sensibility will not be whether some evangelically flavored form of Western cultural pluralism and libertarianism can seriously compete with the moral and spiritual absolutes being propounded by the resurgence of religion throughout the developing world. The challenge is to be able to frame the non-negotiable truth of the Christian witness in terms that will have a genuine, planetary impact, where Christ will become GloboChrist once and for all.

Unfortunately, the issues of the new, trendsetting Emergent Village kind of postmodern Christianity are not really global issues. At the start of the new millennium, they are simply a replay of the modernist-fundamentalist debates of a century ago, with a few savory pinches of the culture wars thrown in for good measure. They are debates over how rigid or loose one is supposed to take classical Christian directives, how far one can accommodate to contemporary secular values and perspectives without diluting the meaning and motivating force of the faith itself. Accommodating or not accommodating to the saeculum is no longer of any discernible consequence for global Christianity. It is the saeculum itself that is everywhere under siege and is crumbling. The saeculum originally was a classical theological notion. It referred not to the age "to come," or the age that we had all better become "used to," but the age that was "passing away" as the kingdom of God established itself on earth and in resplendent majesty. If the saeculum is passing away, as Derrida and others intimate, then it is not because of some temporary historical cycle that will eventually play itself out, comparable to Republicans or Democrats winning control of Congress. It is because the saeculum has now run right up against the eschaton, the latter of which happens to be the limit of the former. The question no longer is whether to have eschatology but which eschatology to have.

The eschatology of Islam is remarkably persuasive in these times as well, and for many more persuasive. The events of 9/11 were neither a blip on the historical screen nor, as initially construed, a mere militant shock that mobilized a nation—as did Pearl Harbor—for the subsequent war on terror. The phrase "war on terror" has turned out to be a pseudo-war, because it consists in a misapplication of martial and nationalistic sentiment to confront what has turned out to be a still-invisible global fault line between two eschatological visions that are gripping more and more of humankind. The Christian West—in its privatized middle-class cocoon of consumerist self-indulgence, fortified with all the politically correct opinions, and indulging in what the Dutch, borrowing from the French, call being *satisfait*—has assumed that eschatology is no longer relevant. After all, why do we need a new heaven and a new earth when people who have historically hated one another can now learn to love one another through podcasting? But eschatology is increasingly relevant to Hardt and Negri's multitudes, whose hand-to-mouth existence in the shanty towns of the planetary slums leaves little time to worry about what next file they are going to download.

As Gilles Kepel notes, the economic chasm between the neo-capitalist West and the postcolonial developing South has made the rejection of secular liberalism and its worldly utopias, even if it espouses political solidarity with the downtrodden, a burgeoning trend. What Derrida calls the "resurgence of religion" Kepel dubs "the revenge of God." This revenge is most evident in what Kepel labels the "re-Islamization" of both the Middle East and the Muslim ethnic communities of urban Europe. "The re-Islamization movements have demonstrated their skill at expressing a social problem in religious terms."[9] Muslim apocalypticism draws strongly on the eschatology of the Mahdist traditions, which are not found in the Qur'an itself and are therefore becoming a prevalent, if not quite yet dominant, factor in shaping Islamist internationalism.

As David Cook concludes, "There is an intense desire to be rid of the politically fragmented Muslim present—and a tendency to blame this condition on the West." As a matter of course, according to Cook, Muslim apocalypticism has built into its regime of discourse the assumption that righteous Islam is battling a world conspiracy of Jewry, abetted by the United States; this dangerous fantasy not only has startling similarities to Nazism but because of its widespread appeal it may also be even more virulent. Furthermore, Muslim militancy is increasingly committed to "regain[ing] the mythical Islamic unity of classical time in preparation for the end of the world."[10]

9. Gilles Kepel, *The Revenge of God: The Resurgence of Islam, Christianity, and Judaism in the Modern World*, trans. Alan Braley (University Park: Pennsylvania State University Press, 1994), 45.

10. David Cook, *Contemporary Muslim Apocalyptic Literature* (Syracuse, NY: Syracuse University Press, 2005), 227.

Re-Islamization is not a simple aberration of unenlightened fundamentalists, who can be ultimately assimilated through engagement, the addressing of grievances, and smart diplomacy into an
Occidentalist cosmopolitan world state of the variety Kant and
Derrida have dreamed of. The only real choice right now is between
this apocalyptic fantasy on one hand, for which secular liberalism
is no match anyway, and a new eschatological fervor on the part of
Christians the world over on the other, particularly in the senescent
West, that will reactivate the summons of the Great Commission in
these latter days. Can we commit ourselves to preaching the joyful
inevitability of the coming GloboChrist, the GloboChrist who turns
back the sword of Islam just as Pope Leo in the fifth century, according to the Christian legend, turned back Attila, the "Scourge of
God," at the River Po through the power of God and his miraculous
sign in the heavens? Or is the "emerging" future of the new evangelical Christianity, as Mark Driscoll has savagely and sarcastically
quipped, in the hands of a generation of "whiny idealists getting
together in small groups to complain about megachurches and the
religious right rather than doing something" that will hasten the
eschaton itself?[11]

11. Mark Driscoll, in "Seven Big Questions," *Relevant Magazine* 24 (January-February 2007): 75.

A Concluding
Unacademic Postscript

> If you board the wrong train, it is no use running
> along the corridor in the other direction.
> Dietrich Bonhoeffer

After Postmodernism

Even though in the global context we have now all entered the postmodern age, the debate in the West over postmodernism as a philosophy, worldview, or lifestyle—even a Christian postmodernism—is winding down. One might say that we are now, at least in terms of the utility of the conversation itself, already postpomo. We are fast approaching a time that comes after postmodernism. We are in an even stranger epoch than the post-1960s one that inaugurated postmodernism. The epoch might be awkwardly lyricized as "post-post-postmodern," but that is simply heaping hyphen upon hyphen and bandying about pointless neologisms.

During the 1980s and early 1990s, the debate over whether postmodernism boded well or ill raged largely in the American university and was often viewed with wry bemusement by editorial writers, social critics, and haut monde cultural analysts, especially those who commandeered the pages of the *New York Review of*

Books. Toward the end of the 1990s the secular controversy had exhausted itself, yet American evangelicals, who in the past could never have been accused of "going pomo," suddenly revived the argument with abandon. Postmodern Christianity was later to be renamed the "emerging church movement" as part of a deliberate promotional ploy by a group of new theological progressives led by Brian McLaren; it suddenly was all the rage. As in the 1980s, no one was sure exactly what they were wrangling about, but everyone quickly took sides for or against the postmodernist phenomenon. And as happened in its previous incarnation, the controversy was pockmarked with excessive sloganeering and a lot of nasty name-calling.

As I reported in my book *The Next Reformation: Why Evangelicals Must Embrace Postmodernity*, published in 2004, the name-calling itself was fueled by a curious tendency on the part of evangelical academics simply to rename their old, familiar demons. During the age of Francis Schaeffer, from approximately the beginnings of the Kennedy presidency to the early 1970s, when the evangelical worldview was both challenged and threatened by the gospel of Christian atheism and the new death-of-God theologies, the most awful bogey—the true *hostis generis humani* (enemy of humankind)—was something called secular humanism. Whatever secular humanism was—and it was never clear exactly what it was—it was bad, and it was bad because it was the opposite of the Christian worldview. Schaeffer had his own vocabulary for this popular demonology. The most prominent demons were various abstract "isms"—nihilism, existentialism, relativism, and so forth.

By the time of the Carter presidency, existentialism as the all-encompassing intellectual fashion it had been during the two decades following the Second World War was discarded and forgotten. Throughout its heyday it had been seen as subtly equivalent to the two other variables in the equation: nihilism and relativism. Once postmodernism—a word originally concocted in the mid-1970s to refer to the new eclectic and experimental styles of urban architecture—came to be applied to the kind of avant-garde philosophy that had recently been imported from France in about 1980, all at once the cultural conservatives dominant during the Reagan presidency began using it to identify the same specters that had kept Schaeffer up at night. Now postmodernism meant what existentialism had previously meant. Its synonyms were—you guessed it—nihilism and relativism.

To this day it is not at all clear why the cultural old guard began using the word *postmodernism* to refer to what had in the previous generation had been called *existentialism*. Possibly it was because the two movements came out of France. And France, as it had been for two centuries, was reputedly the source of every form of moral and spiritual depravity that Americans would ever have to fend against. But postmodernism is something far more sweeping and complex than the self-designated intellectual vice squads in the evangelical seminaries can contend with. Railing against postmodernism and exhorting contemporary Christians to eschew it is not much different than urging them to go out of their way to avoid the twenty-first century. The postmodern world is our permanent legacy, just as the Constantinian church became the heritage of Christianity after the fourth century, even though there have been countless theologians for centuries who have rued the day when, after enduring more than three centuries of struggle and persecution, the followers of Jesus fostered the sanctioned faith of the empire.

Who's Afraid of Relativism?

What anti-postmodernists brand as the danger of embracing relativism amounts to nothing more than a refusal to acknowledge the overwhelming fact of cultural heterogeneity and social pluralism after the collapse of the old Christendom. But our globopomo post-Christendom is no more a threat than it is an opportunity for ongoing and amazing triumphs of ministry and the miraculous workings of God. The first apostles and the early Christians faced the same daunting and promiscuous pluralism during the heroic era of pre-Constantinian Christianity. But they were not cowed by it. The streets and bazaars of the boundless *Romanitas* were swarming and teeming with every spiritual commodity and cult of which the mind could conceive, as the well-known second-century picaresque novel *The Golden Ass*, by the Roman writer Apuleius, graphically conveys.

Yet these same Christians did not shrink from stepping out into the same rough-and-tumble scene. Every pagan festival or philosophical debate was an opportunity to indigenize the Gospel, as the story of Paul at the Areopagus in Athens underscores (Acts 17). The early Christians were confronted by relativism at every corner, but they relativized the relativists and showed that all these relativities had one common center of gravity—the one God who had revealed himself in the one Christ, whose followers confessed him simply as "Lord."

How did the first evangelists manage relativism? First, they did not inveigh against it; they co-opted it. They did not condemn the swarms of non-Christians, comprising 99.999 percent of everyone they encountered, who were adrift in the relativistic culture of their time. The Jewish and particularly the Pharisaic response was to avoid that culture because of the peril of impurity and pollution, which unfortunately happens to be the counsel these days of so many evangelical theologians. The early Christians waded shoulder-deep into the currents and tides of cultural relativism in order to let God transform the iniquity of gentile heathenism into the original "generous orthodoxy"—as Brian McLaren would put it—of the early church.

When it came to cultural style, Paul did not go around in clear Christian dress. He was something of a covert operator. He wanted to show that the relativity of proliferating spiritual viewpoints could be captured in the net of the gospel itself and turned into the presence of a Christ in which there was "no east or west." In his practice of incarnational ministry, Paul went to them wherever they were, whatever they believed, whatever foreign language they spoke, whatever their strange set of practices.

> For though I am free with respect to all, I have made myself a slave to all, so that I might win more of them. To the Jews I became as a Jew, in order to win Jews. To those under the law I became as one under the law (though I myself am not under the law) so that I might win those under the law. To those outside the law I became as one outside the law (though I am not free from God's law but am under Christ's law) so that I might win those outside the law. To the weak I became weak, so that I might win the weak. I have become all things to all people, that I might by all means save some. I do it all for the sake of the gospel, so that I may share in its blessings. (1 Cor. 9:19–23 NRSV)

No one whose life has been transformed by the power of the risen Christ need fret about being seduced by relativism. A young man passionately in love with his young wife does not need to be warned that there are numerous other women out there who might catch his eye, although that temptation will assuredly arise later as his ardor cools. Similarly, someone on fire with the love of Christ is not going to start fooling around with a miscellany of faith alternatives. There is nothing to distract such a person. That does not mean that there is nothing inherently seductive about relativism. One needs to realize that relativism is not something given that can simply be taken for granted, or dismissed, as much as it is a cleverly honed and often misleading philosophical position.

The relativistic formulation, first epitomized conceptually in the reputed saying of the ancient Greek sophist Protagoras that "man is the measure of all things," is more problematic than its detractors will admit. Protagoras himself merely wanted to come to terms with the empirical fact that people describe things differently from their own observational perch, as in the proverbial question of whether the glass is half empty or half full. Protagoras was a skeptic. He was dubious that objective reality had any significance apart from the fluctuating descriptions we employ. On that score he was not much different from many other great philosophers, including Immanuel Kant and Ludwig Wittgenstein. Protagoras was basically arguing for what philosophers call a perspectivalist view. A hard-core relativist—the guy with the black hat and curling mustache that old-style fundamentalist polemics are always trotting out before the audience for constant booing and hissing—takes one step beyond perspectivalism and asserts that one position is simply as valid as another.

But when it comes to moral and religious questions, there really are few dyed-in-the-wool relativists. A pure relativist would say that one view is as good as another, but practically that is rarely true. Most people hold to a certain view strongly, but they allow other people also to hold their own view. That is what we call tolerance, an ethical disposition that is absolutely crucial in a pluralistic society. What fundamentalism actually means by relativism is the kind of practical tolerance that abounds everywhere—as it should and of legal necessity must—in American culture. Most fundamentalist bashing of postmodernism has nothing to do with postmodernism as either a philosophical or cultural development. Nor does it amount to a meaningful critique of shoddy conceptual thinking and the lack of genuine spiritual conviction nowadays, which is rampant and probably always has been.

The attack on relativism depends on the fabrication of a straw man. It secretly signifies the fundamentalist outrage that their view of religiosity is shared less and less by the public at large, that they have failed to persuade anybody except their own minions, and that non-Christians are allowed to immigrate and believe whatever they want without constraint or coercion. Are Christian believers in Africa relativists because they happen to be convinced as a matter of course that people are resurrected from the dead every day, although most Western religious rationalists would call that superstition? They consider themselves Christians as fiercely as American fundamentalists count themselves Christians, and after all they do have Scripture to back up their "irrational" belief.

Fundamentalists detest postmodernist thinking, which they dismiss as relativist thinking, because they are really seeking to shut their eyes and magically wish away the challenge of giving a rational or theological account of their faith, while knowledge and the different strains of religious and ethical discourse proliferate in a global setting. Fundamentalism is, as I have argued in an earlier book, the idolatrous substitution of eighteenth-century propositional rationality for the biblical language of faith itself.[1] This self-delusion is as hard-core as that of the Pharisees in Jesus's time, as can be seen in the tirades of writers like R. Scott Smith. He claims to be defending the gospel against the "heresy" of postmodernism—as if postmodernism were a statement of faith rather than a particular philosophical advance for our generation that can be used either to support or dismiss Christianity, as Aristotle was used in the thirteenth century.

Smith writes: "In sharp contrast to the modern attitudes that we could find absolutely certain truths through universal human reason, postmodernism instead stresses a humility of knowledge, which appeals to postmodern people today."[2] Apparently Smith construes intellectual humility here as somehow un-Christian. He perhaps has decided to ignore the wisdom-and-folly argument in Paul (1 Cor. 1–2). Smith finds redemption in the fight against postmodernism as his own philosophical position, which he labels "epistemological realism," a fancy word for "natural theology," which evangelicals historically have considered inimical to the Christian revelation itself. "Christians should not embrace a postmodern understanding

1. See Carl Raschke, *The Next Reformation: Why Evangelicals Must Embrace Postmodernity* (Grand Rapids: Baker Academic, 2004).
2. R. Scott Smith, *Truth and the New Kind of Christian: The Emerging Effects of Postmodernism in the Church* (Wheaton: Crossway Books, 2005), 61.

of the faith itself. That will lead to disaster, for Christianity cannot survive a transformation into being a construction of our language use. . . . Christians need to stop embracing relativism and even a postmodernization of the faith itself, for those attitudes and actions are adulterous against God. In effect, even if unconsciously, we set ourselves up as being in control, as being able actually to construct God. That is sin and cannot please God."[3]

Fortunately, there is much, much more at stake in the looming eschatological battle than the kinds of theoretical wrangles that were common in Anglo-American philosophy in the early twentieth century. Like most of his confreres, Smith is tilting at windmills and certainly has little grasp or appreciation of what the postmodern philosophical revolution really amounts to. This kind of ignorance is regrettably typical of so many of the academic polemics nowadays that are coming out of the old-line evangelical schools and seminaries. The "transformation" of the language of the gospel into a "construction of our language use" does not describe anything that is happening whatsoever these days. It refers to a move that certain liberal Protestant theologians were making in the 1960s, long before the postmodernist wave that gained strength and momentum in the early 1980s swept them and other datable experiments away. As I have written in *The Next Reformation*, postmodern religious thought is about the deconstruction of the constructionist liberalism that Smith has in mind and wrongly identifies as "pomo," a process of deconstruction that makes straight a highway for authentic, biblical faith.

Furthermore, John MacArthur insists that the issue is of much broader magnitude than "mere semantics or slight philosophical disagreement. The purity of the gospel itself is at stake. If God's Word cannot be understood with certainty, then a saving comprehension of the gospel becomes an impossible task."[4] One is prompted to ask, what exactly is meant by the "purity" of the faith? Smith seems to imply that "purity" is indistinguishable from philosophical clarity and coherence, a distinctly unbiblical and even more idolatrous or adulterous contention. "Blessed are the pure in heart, for they will

3. Ibid., 189.
4. John MacArthur, "Brian McLaren and the Clarity of Scripture (Part V)," *Pulpit Magazine*, December 22, 2006, http://www.sfpulpit.com/2006/12/22/brian-mclaren-and -the-clarity-of-scripture-part-5/.

see God" (Matt. 5:8). Jesus did not say that purity in one's theology was the same as having a clean or pure heart. That was the gist of his quarrel with the doctors of the law. In Christian thought, and historically in evangelical thought, salvation has ultimately been about the heart, not the mind.

The kind of philosophical Pharisaism that has thoroughly infected evangelical theology, prostituting the gospel for the sake of what is a spurious modernist epistemology or philosophical theory of knowledge to begin with, is probably more responsible for the spread of relativism, which has been snowballing for the last half century in the Western world, than any subtle seepage of pomo premises into the cultural and intellectual mainstream. A cheap metaphysical absolutism, derived from seventeenth-century secular philosophy and pretending to be the basis of biblical inerrancy, has spawned as its dialectical opposite an equally cheap and wishy-washy pop principle of moral and social relativity. From God's point of view the "abomination of desolation" in today's culture is not the level of sophistication, or purity, of one's supposed take on how we know what we know, or do not know what we know. That is theological arrogance and self-deception. It is the installation of a swinish and self-congratulatory intellectual faddism, found in both conservative and liberal religion, in the holy temple of the Christian faith. We need to turn over the tables and throw out not only the money changers—the growth gurus who both run and ruin the evangelical churches—but also the traders in conceptual currency who transform God's *ekklēsia* into a brothel of philosophical and cultural fashions rather than a genuine house of prayer; we need to open our hearts and minds into authentic relationship with the Lord.

Neither Right nor Left

The traders lamentably are not only legion on the right but are also increasingly found on the left. A postmodern Christian who wants to stay pure to the gospel needs to navigate carefully, not running off the road into the ditch on either side. In American Christianity much of the debate about modern and postmodern, conventional and emerging, has degenerated into just one more skirmish in the ongoing culture wars, with unmistakable political overtones mimicking familiar campaign bluster. The leadership of the emerging movement has increasingly pushed the discourse from what it might mean to follow Jesus to what it might mean to follow the policy agenda of the Democratic National Committee. If the criticism of the now-fading religious right was that one cannot make Jesus into a Republican, it is equally true that one cannot simply convert him into a Democrat.

It is true that what we somewhat crudely call modernist evangelicalism—we don't talk much about the "fundies" any more, mainly because we know fundamentalist Islam is much worse—needs to be put to rest for its narrow-mindedness, legalism, exclusivity, and idolatry. But it is just as true that what we are—again crudely—calling postmodernist evangelicalism has many of the same flaws. Open-mindedness, nonjudgmentalism, and radical inclusivity are no less idolatrous. In many respects the emerging religious left is just a fun-house mirror of the religious right; it is defined by its spirit of contrariness and a kind of passive-aggressive incredulity about what is lurking out there in the world at large. The culture wars are of no more consequence for the coming GloboChristianity than the burning of Bibles in India by Hindu nationalists is for a typical rural church in Ohio. They are simply our own homegrown version of what we in the rest of the planet cavalierly refer to as sectarian strife. They are more evidence that God has written or is getting ready to write "Ichabod" (the glory has departed; 1 Sam. 4:21) on the sanctuary of American Christianity unless it repents and turns to the Lord.

It was the American aphorist Mason Cooley who once quipped that he was always "open-minded" about that which he cared nothing about. A personal friend of mine, noting the now-hackneyed slogan of certain political parties that they wanted to be a "big tent" under which any act in the circus could perform, also quipped: "The bigger the tent, the more likely it is to catch the wind and blow down." That may be true from an engineering standpoint, but it points to the hollowness of all forms of radical inclusivity. The more inclusive you are, the less you really stand for anything that anyone can recognize, and the less likely people are to be committed to what you espouse once the weather changes. Postmodernism—a somewhat slippery "ism" that should not be confused with modernity, which connotes nothing more than our current historical estate—has a reputation for a hypertolerant and indiscriminate acceptance of everything happening in our culture. The reputation is not altogether undeserved, although use of the term in this way fosters the false impression that postmodern thought and philosophy, which at one time was chided by liberals in the early days for being too exclusivistic, is virtually the same as postmodern culture.

Perhaps the most widely read and influential book that promotes the gospel of inclusivity is Brian McLaren's *A Generous Orthodoxy*, published about the same time as *The Next Reformation*. Although McLaren and I know each other well, have worked together on sundry projects, and have both ridden the same wave, we seem to have ended up in different places. McLaren is probably more misunderstood than I am. And both of us are constantly being attacked by ultrarightists in the church, who never bother to read what either of us actually writes and count us as a fifth column designed to corrode and undermine the steel solidity of genuine evangelical Christianity, whatever that might be. McLaren's influence has been enormous, which has also been overly and largely for the good, inasmuch as the emerging church he has inspired has played a mighty role in breaking down the rigidities and fixities of fundamentalist Christianity, which—as Islamism does for Islam—betrays the gospel by confusing ideology with faith.

But McLaren does exhibit a vulnerability that needs to be sedulously and prayerfully pondered by those who are giddy to believe that a new kind of Christian is simply an easier-to-get-along-with Christian. The difference between McLaren and me may come down to the fact that I am a product of what was called the Magisterial Reformation, championed by Luther, Calvin, Zwingli, and others, and he is an admitted product of the Radical Reformation, propelled by the Anabaptists. The Anabaptists rejected all learning and clerical training as a condition of spiritual authority, which is characteristic of the emerging movement as it gathers steam. The Radical Reformers, who considered Scripture authoritative only when it conformed to one's own inner conscience, were as a rule more "inclusive" than their Magisterial counterparts.

McLaren is vulnerable on what inclusivity as the dominant strategy for kingdom promotion might mean in practical terms. In his book he lays out a whole laundry list of attributions that the garden-variety pastor, or theologue, would consider utterly contradictory. The subtitle, a mind-boggler, reads as follows: "Why I am a missional + evangelical + post/protestant + liberal/conservative + charismatic/ contemplative + fundamentalist/Calvinist + Anabaptist/Anglican

+ methodist + catholic + green + incarnational + depressed-yet-hopeful + emergent + unfinished Christian." Assumedly this string of paradoxes deconstructs the tendency that Protestant Christians have always had to identify the truth of the faith as a whole with their special doctrinal statement of the truth, or their forms of praxis. McLaren rightly observes that these strains of Christianity all add up to the larger picture of who Jesus was and is and what he calls us to.

In his chapter on why he is incarnational, McLaren even goes so far as to welcome into his "generous orthodoxy" the non-Christian religions of the world. McLaren denies that we must be inclusive of other religions because, contrary to the trite sophism, "all religions say the same thing." But in many ways he also wants to point beyond what we normally mean by "Christian" to an inclusive world spirituality of mutual tolerance, dialogue, and respect, perhaps similar to different clothing or culinary styles. "I am more and more convinced that Jesus didn't come merely to start another religion to compete in the marketplace of other religions. If anything, I believe he came to end standard competitive religion (which Paul called 'the law') by fulfilling it; I believe he came to open up something beyond religion —a new possibility, a realm, a domain, a territory of the spirit that welcomes everyone but requires everyone (now including members of the Christian religion) to think again and become like little children."[5]

In the history of religions, this je ne sais quoi, this mysterious and slippery "something beyond religion," is often referred to as perennialism, esotericism, Gnosticism, New Age religion, and so forth. It is the "truth in you" that for the most part cannot be articulated. Within that galaxy are even forms of esoteric Christianity, a prime example of which is in the Gnostic Gospels on which the movie *The Da Vinci Code* claimed to be based. In the history of the church, it was the struggle against Gnosticism during the second century out of which what we now dub "orthodoxy" emerged. Gnosticism, even though to this day it remains historically opaque, has always been an appealing option for Christians angry and confused by all the competing claims of sectarian Christianity. If Christians cannot agree on the truth, the Gnostic protests, then I will just find the

5. Brian McLaren, *A Generous Orthodoxy* (Grand Rapids: Zondervan, 2004), 266.

truth in my own soul, or inner light. The Radical Reformation of
the sixteenth century had a definite Gnostic flavor, although it was
unlike ancient Gnosticism in being communitarian (not individualistic) and oriented toward social action and good works. I assume
that is where McLaren is ultimately coming from.

In a later book McLaren actually uses language of esotericism in
exhorting us to understand what we might call the "Jesus secret."
He does not have in mind anything titillating, scandalous, or even
baldly heretical. But the comparison is more than incidental. In
The Secret Message of Jesus, which sounds a little like the "secret
gospels" of the Gnostics, McLaren characterizes the kingdom of
God as something we see primarily for ourselves on the "inside" of
things. "These moments of seeing—these glimpses of insight into the
kingdom—can't be conjured or created. They can only be received.
And similarly the kingdom itself—what 'the world wants to be and
is preparing to be'—can't be achieved, but only received."[6] After
reading the book we have little sense of the Jesus secret other than
that it is a secret. If one matches that motif with the argument of *A
Generous Orthodoxy*, it becomes clear that emerging church theology
is an inkblot test for whatever we see in it, or want to see in it.

Burger King Christianity

Although McLaren clearly and consciously would not want to
go there, one must ask if this rendering does not open the door to
a sanctification of what we already have even in modernist Christianity, an evangelical spiritual consumerism that is merely a more
sophisticated form of Burger King Christianity. The struggle in
second-century Christianity with secret, or esoteric, Christianity
is often misunderstood by many scholars, let alone laypeople. The
struggle is often pitched in terms of Gnostic heresy versus orthodoxy. According to popular accounts, based on the kinds of historical fabrications and distortions found in books like *The Da
Vinci Code*, Gnosticism was the dynamic and emerging strain of
the new Christianity that began at Jesus's resurrection, and somehow the established church through political intrigue, machination,

6. Brian McLaren, *The Secret Message of Jesus* (Nashville: Thomas Nelson, 2006),
266.

and intimidation succeeded in squelching it. Thus the casual reader today has the impression that second-century Christians were given a Hobson's choice between Gnosticism and what would eventually become Roman Catholic orthodoxy, which won out in the end only because it was more adept at power politics. This interpretation fits a popular twenty-first-century view of how religion in general is supposed to operate and has its origins in nineteenth-century Marxist and materialist critiques of historical Christianity. It also goes along with the romantic or countercultural ideal prevalent today that the true faith has somehow been in a guerilla conflict with the ecclesiastical powers that be.

But the picture is flawed and does not fit the second century, about which little is actually known anyway. In its different historical guises, Gnosticism has always represented the breakdown of the church as the body of Christ, as the *sanctorum communio*, "community of saints," and the turn toward a radically privatized spirituality, what the ancient esoteric philosopher Plotinus dubbed "the flight of the alone to the Alone." Today's eclectic spiritualism, even in its Christian variations, is simply a cockier and more self-important subset of globalized consumption, which promises anything anytime to anyone so long as it is enjoyable, satisfying, and undemanding. Just as the second-century church was fighting against Gnosticism, the Burger King Christianity of its own day and age, so today we are confronted with a GloboAntichrist in the form of a self-blinkered "have it your way" mentality, buttressed by an uncritical obsession with openness that ignores Jesus's demands of discipleship. This uniquely Western consumer Gnosticism not only lacks the transformative power of the gospel of Jesus Christ; it also cannot and will not beard the forces arrayed against the coming kingdom of God. To be incarnational in the most radical and eschatological sense, as we need to understand it, is diametrically opposite to Burger King Christianity. It is not the waving of the white flag by God's warriors in preparation for a total surrender to the powers of the saeculum and its privatized sensibilities, as the radical theologians of the late 1960s first proclaimed and as their new millennial imitators, who seem to have grossly misappropriated the term "postmodern," are beginning to suggest with similar rhetoric.

Much of the revival of this trend toward a 1960s-style secular theology can be traced to Gianni Vattimo's influence. Vattimo's concept of a "weak Christianity," first tendered in his 2002 book

After Christianity, has undergirded the trend. Vattimo, moving in a direction different from Derrida, understands the "return" of religion in a historically progressive and irenic manner of speaking. In crucial respects this weak Christianity signifies a return to nineteenth-century liberalism, albeit from a postcolonial vantage point. In effect, Vattimo regards twenty-first-century European-style multiculturalism as the apex of historical development. He looks on the "course of history as driven toward emancipation by diminishing strong structures (in thought, individual consciousness, political power, social relations, and religion)" as indeed "a transcription of the Christian message of the incarnation of God, which Saint Paul also calls kenosis—that is, the abasement, humiliation, and weakening of God."[7]

Nietzsche's vision of the "death of God" was really the apprehension of modern multicultural secularism, Vattimo blithely argues in a rather ridiculous reading of what Nietzsche really meant. Nietzsche did not, by the way, construe the death of God as any sort of agreeable development. Rather, he regarded the death of God as a devastating, though inevitable, event that was destined to shake European civilization to its foundations, which indeed turned out to be what happened. "Postmodern faith," in this pseudo-Nietzschean account according to Vattimo, is liberation from all forms of authority, including scriptural and clerical authority, and the exploration of preferences, options, and differences. It is no longer founded on belief but on "believing that one believes."

Nor does Christianity have any "answers" other than paying attention to what others have to say, or where others might be "coming from." The ever-present danger is always intolerance and fundamentalism. "In the Babel-like world of pluralism, cultural and religious identities are destined to move toward fanaticism unless they explicitly develop a spirit of weakness."[8] The spirit of weakness— what Vattimo elsewhere terms "weak thought" in general—entails an ethic of nonjudgmental noncommitment. "In intercultural or interreligious dialogue, this signifies acknowledging that the other might be right," which is tantamount to true Christian "charity." It is also, Vattimo claims, the same as Christianity's "universalizing

7. Gianni Vattimo, *After Christianity*, trans. Luca D'Isanto (New York: Columbia University Press, 2002), 91.
8. Ibid., 100.

function." "If Christian identity, applying the principle of charity, takes the shape of hospitality in dialogue between religions and cultures, it must limit itself entirely to listening, and thus giving voice to the guests."[9]

If Nietzsche is Vattimo's inspiration, then the latter remark should be taken as tongue in cheek. One of the most compelling passages in Nietzsche's posthumously published writings edited under the title of *The Will to Power* runs as follows: "Nihilism stands at the door: whence comes this uncanniest of all guests?"[10] As both Nietzsche and Heidegger understood, nihilism is not an uninvited guest. In fact, nihilism is the blood relation to modernist Christian theology, what Nietzsche termed the "Christian-moral view of the world." Nihilism stands at the door because it wants to come into its own house, which does not acknowledge it. Nihilism is the dirty little secret of all liberal theologies and all liberal politics. It is also the dirty little secret of all fundamentalist and dogmatic theologies, and their so-called conservative politics, which after a while lose their sense of conviction and turn liberal. If one reads most of the rhetoric of the emerging church these days, it seems to have lost both its radicality and vitality. The emerging movement, ever critical of the idolatrous identification of mainstream American evangelicalism with rightist politics, has apparently become a receptacle for left-wing or progressive politics without exerting any of the critical distance that a genuine kingdom-of-God perspective would demand.

But both conservatism and liberalism are simply competing versions of the same modernist epistemology, which has now disclosed its nihilistic underbelly. "What does nihilism mean? *That the highest values devaluate themselves*. The aim is lacking; 'why' finds no answer."[11] One cannot speak confidently of the presence of Christ and the teachings of Christ because not only does the "Why?" find no answer but the question seems confused and problematic in the first place.

In other words, the collapse of the kingdom-of-God proclamation into a social gospel preoccupied with social issues leads to a loss of the sense of majesty and transcendence that infuses both the

9. Ibid., 101.
10. Friedrich Nietzsche, *The Will to Power*, trans. Walter Kaufmann (New York: Random House, 1967), 7.
11. Ibid., 9, emphasis in original.

faith relationship between God and the believer and the relational truth of all relationships, which the Great Commandment and the ideal of the *sanctorum communio* necessitate. The reduction of the Great Commission to movement politics preoccupied with school prayer, abortion, and preventing gay marriage is scarcely challenged and critiqued by reducing the Great Commission to movement politics preoccupied with ending war, increasing funding for the homeless, and legitimating gay marriage. Vattimo's "weak Christianity" could easily be construed as nothing more than a "resentful" (Nietzsche's term) version of the new bobo pseudo-gospel of personal self-fulfillment and moral self-importance that has been so characteristic of this generation of vipers that we know as the baby boomers. The coming of GloboChristianity under the sovereign rule of the GloboChrist means that this bobo pseudo-gospel, whether it has a traditional or progressive coloration, must be cast aside in the same way that ancient Gnosticism was cast aside.

The Christian South is not populated by the self-tortured intellectuals who have distorted the discourse in our Western post-Christian Christiana. Nor is it driven by the corporate consumerism that has equally distorted both church message and church organization. The rise of the Christian South, as far as the church is concerned (and we do not have the new politically correct emerging orthodoxy in mind), is the real postmodern moment. It is the global postmodern (or what we have coyly termed *globopomo*) moment. The current "bobopomo" wave in the West, which has been rolling along in a sort of retrorevival of 1960s-style cultural angst, is about to crash against the rock of historical reality.

The Indian summer of the secular West is over. A cold and furious storm is boiling across the horizon. At this writing Islamism, with its own apocalyptic courage of conviction, is gathering strength as well as converts. Even after 9/11 the West refuses to comprehend it and lacks the will to confront it. The boboists, as Jeremiah sarcastically reports, "cry 'Peace, peace,' when there is no peace" (Cf. Jer. 6:14; 8:11 KJV). As the intellectual spear-carriers of the West, they are no different and no more heroic than Jehoiakim. They cannot speak for the West because they do not know what it is or what it means anymore or even who God is. They are tormented by what Roger Scruton terms a "down with us mentality" that constitutes a "culture of repudiation," renouncing the "cultural inheritance that defines us as something distinct from the rest."[12] But Christ knows his own.

The Communion of Saints, or GloboEschatology

Christ's "own" is the church. The postmodern church can no longer foster its identity merely in a Western countercultural guise, for a counterculture is still a particularist culture. Indeed, it is just a subculture that mirrors darkly what it has set its face against. The stakes are too high, much too high. Wandering in the wide-open "smooth spaces" of globalization, the postmodern church must no longer take its cues from the twilight broodings of the West or from the American culture wars. It must become the incarnational church that knows no cultural boundaries. It must become the global body of the GloboChrist, the shining bride waiting on her groom and standing fast in the promise "until the appearing of our Lord Jesus Christ, which God will bring about in his own time—God, the blessed and only Ruler, the King of kings and Lord of lords, who alone is immortal and who lives in unapproachable light, whom no one has seen or can see" (1 Tim. 6:14–16).

For a more cultivated "theological" insight about what this move might truly mean, we might take note of the reflections of the great twentieth-century Christian theologian Dietrich Bonhoeffer, whose in-the-trenches defense of the church against the jackbooted juggernaut of Nazism may have some applications for an age that is sailing into a comparable time of crisis. In his masterful treatise on the meaning of the *sanctorum communio*, Bonhoeffer writes that "Christian eschatology is essentially the eschatology of the church." It is an eschatology involving the church's "consummation."[13] The word *church* has been bandied about ad nauseum, particularly in Western theology. Frequently the church is construed, in a sort of bare-bones Augustinian style, as the visible representative of the

12. Roger Scruton, *The West and the Rest: Globalization and the Terrorist Threat* (Wilmington, DE: Intercollegiate Studies Institute, 2002), 73. See also Philip D. Curtin, *The World and the West: The European Challenge and the Overseas Response in the Age of Empire* (Cambridge: Cambridge University Press, 2000); Philippe Nemo, *What Is the West?* trans. Kenneth Casler (Pittsburgh: Duquesne University Press, 2004).

13. Dietrich Bonhoeffer, *The Communion of Saints: A Dogmatic Inquiry into the Sociology of the Church* (New York: Harper & Row, 1960), 199.

eternal order, the *civitas Dei*. The corruptibility and fallibility of
the church in its Augustinian-Protestant modality has in the past
several centuries become an excuse for the enduring ineffectual-
ity and irrelevance of the church. Who needs the church when we
can all have our own custom-designed and individualized style of
spirituality?

The church can never be relevant, however, when it seeks mainly to
be attractive to a particular focus group or demographic constituency.
It can only be relevant when it is the catholic church, as confessed in
the Apostles' Creed. But what would the genuine catholicity of the
church signify in the globopomo moment of history, when all preten-
sions to cultural and religious uniformity, or hegemony, are shattered
by the rampant transformation of the economies and social fabrics
of the planet en masse? It cannot be Roman catholicity. It cannot be
a worldwide orthodoxy, whatever that might connote. It cannot be
"radical orthodoxy." It cannot be Protestant privatistic and pietistic
catholicity, which has degenerated into consumerist seeker sensitiv-
ity. It cannot be the curious kind of urban café catholicity distilled
from unremitting conversation and hospitality along the lines of
Vattimo's "weak Christianity." It cannot be some pseudo-global
and premillennial fundamentalist utopia that is faithful neither to
the authority of Scripture nor to the Great Commission and the
Great Commandment.

Bonhoeffer himself hints at such a genuine postmodern and global
catholicity. Although Bonhoeffer uses the philosophically dated
language of the *Existenz-Philosophie* (existence philosophy) and
the personalist idealism of the first half of the twentieth century,
his insights need to be renewed with vigor, insofar as the cultural
libertarianism, moral latitudinarianism, and "multitudinism" of
the present era are not merely inadequate but have also become
bankrupt. For Bonhoeffer, the "communion of saints" is the community of persons in profound and God-centered and God-inflamed
relationship with one another, where the revelation of the other is the
revelation of the holy, and vice versa. "For the concepts of person,
community, and God have an essential and indissoluble relation to
one another."[14] Buber's so-called I-Thou relationship, where interpersonal relationships can never be reduced to mere social relationships because they constitute an indescribable and unquantifiable

14. Ibid., 22.

encounter with the "wholly Other" in the face of the Other (language that postdates Bonhoeffer and derives from the work of Emmanuel Lévinas, a Jew), also heavily informs the latter's vision.

The globochurch of the GloboChrist is the presence of the Christ in the true and unshakable *communio* where we are all Christs to one another. If in that community we are Christs to one another, then we are on the way to becoming authentically the church of the consummation, which reaches its own eschatological fulfillment when Christ comes. There is no power in this world, the world that is the saeculum—no militant jihad, no cultural coup de main engineered by any fundamentalism, no liberal double-speak and double-mindedness—that can prevent a second coming, the advent of the GloboChrist in this momentous sense.

For quite a while there has been silence in heaven. But already the sky is flashing. "I saw heaven standing open and there before me was a white horse, whose rider is called Faithful and True. With justice he judges and makes war. His eyes are like blazing fire, and on his head are many crowns. He has a name written on him that no one knows but he himself knows" (Rev. 19:11–12).

What is this name? It is the unbearable and indecipherable name, the name of the global conqueror, as the passage tells us: "King of kings and Lord of lords" (Rev. 19:16). We are talking about parousia, the coming of the GloboChrist in power and great glory. It is now up to the saints to be watchful and ready.

"Yes, I am coming soon." Amen. Come, Lord Jesus.

Index

Abbasid Empire, 141
Abrahamic promise, 98–102
Acton, David, 85–86
African Christianity, 24–25, 25n3, 43–44, 69
After Christianity (Vattimo), 163–64
Ahmadinejad, Mahmoud, 140–41
Ahmed, Akbar, 113–14
al-Qaida. *See* Qaida, al-
American Christianity, 119–20, 158–59
Anabaptist movement, 26n5, 88, 160
ancestor worship, 70
Asherahs, 107
Asian Christianity, 55–56
Augustine of Hippo, 71, 114–15
Austrian Baptist Union, 87–91

Baals, 107
Baaz, Abd-al-Aziz ibn Abd Allah ibn, 104
baby boomers, 166
Baptist movement, in Europe, 87–88
Barber, Benjamin, 76
Bar Kokhba revolt, 136–37
Barth, Karl, 92
Baudrillard, Jean, 28
Benedict XVI, Pope, 92–93
bin Laden, Osama, 30, 97, 103–6, 128
biosemiotics, 72

bobo (bohemian bourgeois) culture, 51, 166
Bonhoeffer, Dietrich, 92, 132, 144–47, 167–68
Bosnian conflict, 113
Bright Future News Agency, 139
Brooks, David, 51
Buddhism, 83–84, 143
Burger King Christianity, 119, 162–63
buzz marketing, 60

Chestnut, R. Andrew, 54
Chinese Christianity, 24
Christian Community Action, 45–46
Christianity
    Christianization of developing countries, 24–25, 43–46
    as cultural force in West, 24
    and globalization, 31–32
    Great Commission, 47–51, 62
    indigenization, 39–46, 69–70
    and mystery religions, 80–84
    relevance of, 52–56
    spread, in Roman era, 77–78
    weakness, vs. Islam, 107–15
    See also evangelical Christianity; GloboChristianity
"Christ of culture," 26

171

church, 167–69
civil rights movement, 82
Cohn, Norman, 137–38
Cold War, 29, 34
Colossians, Paul's Epistle to, 63–66
Communism, collapse of, 76, 127
The Communist Manifesto (Marx), 125
communitarianism, 126
Constantinian age, 33
contextualization, 50–51, 54–55, 58, 60–62
Cook, David, 149
Cooley, Mason, 159
Corten, André, 68
Cratylus (Plato), 117
Crosspointe Community Church, 44–46
culture, evangelical engagement with, 56–63
culture wars, 23–24, 158–59

Dar al-Islam, 95, 96, 106
Darby, Charles, 135
death-of-God movement, 37–38, 131, 164
Deleuze, Gilles, 28, 39–40, 41, 68–69, 121–22
Derrida, Jacques, 33–35, 67, 144
deterritorialization, 28–29
developing countries, Christianization of,
       24–25, 42–46
dhimmitude, 95
discipleship, 132–33
Donnan, Hastings, 113–14

Eleusinian mysteries, 80
emerging church movement, 51, 54–55,
       152, 158–59
Engels, Friedrich, 138
Esau, 99
eschatology
   Christian, 142–43, 167–69
   Christian vs. Muslim, 143–50
   history of theme of, 135–38
   Mahdism, 134–35, 139–43
   messianism and globalization, 138–43
   pop, 134
Europe, Western
   Christianity no longer cultural force in,
       23–24, 42–43
   deterritorialization of, 29
   missionizing in, 84–93
   modernist Eurocentrism, 27

evangelical Christianity
   Burger King Christianity, 119, 162–63
   and cultural engagement, 56–58
   discipleship, 132–33
   inclusivity, 159–62
   and mission work, 58–60
   postmodern and global, 116–27
   and relativism, 153–58
   rhizomic distribution, 123–27
   spirit of weakness in, 163–66
   success and rise of, 37, 39
   See also GloboChristianity
Evangelical Presbyterian Church, 44
existentialism, 152
experimentalism, in American Christianity,
       119–20

Fellowship of Joy, 89
Fischer-Dorl, Dietrich, 87
flat world, 30, 35–36
Friedman, Thomas, 30, 35–36
Frost, Ellen, 27
Frost, Michael, 48, 50
fundamentalism, 57–58, 156

Gemeinschaft, 86
A Generous Orthodoxy (McLaren), 160,
       162
geopolitics, 124–25
Germany, 86–87
globalatinization, 33, 36
globalization
   Christianity as reaction to, 44
   geopolitics of, 124–27
   global polycentrism, 27
   and messianism, 138–43
   and new Pentecostalism, 68
   origins and first inroads of, 38–39
   and postmodernism, 28–32
   privatism vs. collectivism in, 127–31
   of religion, 29
   religious component of, 76–77
global postmodern Christianity. *See*
       GloboChristianity
GloboChristianity
   about, 23–26
   characteristics of, 39–46, 121, 166
   eschatology of, 168–69

Gnosticism, 80, 161–63
Great Commission, 47–51, 62
Gulf War, 113
Guru Maharaj Ji, 38

Hagar, 98, 99
Hardt, Michael, 123–25
Hare Krishna, 38
Hasan, Muhammad ibn, 139
hermeneutics, biblical, 71
Hirsch, Alan, 48, 50
historical-critical criticism, 79
Hope for Sevilla, 85
House Bethel, 89
Hubmaier, Balthasar, 87–88
Huntington, Samuel, 32, 33

incarnational Christianity
    about, 50–51
    contextualization, 54–55, 58
    and evangelicism, 60–66
    semiotics in, 72–73
inclusivity, 159–62
Indian Christianity, 24
indigenization
    about, 39–46
    embracing, 153–54
    and Gospel's message, 74–80
    and syncretism, 69–70
Internet, 69, 122
Iranian Islamic Revolution, 39, 128, 140
Iraq War, 113
Isaac, 99, 100
Ishmael, 98–99
Islam
    and Christian missionizing, 94–96
    current conflict with, 96–98, 109–15,
        149–50
    and globalization, 108–9
    and Israel, 103–6
    Mahdism, 134–35, 139–43, 149
    in Middle Ages, 95
    Qutb's manifesto for, 127–31
    revelational differences with Judaism
        and Christianity, 98–102
    revelation in, 98–102
    revival of, 30, 32, 37, 38–39, 129–30
    rhizomic growth of, 45–46
    violence and, 130–31

Islam, Globalization, and Postmodernity
    (Ahmed and Donnan), 113
Islamic Brotherhood, 38–39
Israel, State of, 100–101, 103–6

Jacob, 99
jahiliyyists, 106, 128
Jenkins, Jerry, 135
Jenkins, Philip, 58, 81, 85
Jesus Christ
    and eschatology, 142–43
    as Messiah, 70
    radicalness of, 116–17
    as Son of Man, 60–62
Jihad, 76–77
John of Leiden, 138
Judaism, origins of, 98–102

Kentucky Fried Chicken (KFC), 28
Kepel, Gilles, 149
Khomeini, Ayatollah Ruhollah, 140
King, Martin Luther, Jr., 81–82
Klimt, Walter and Andrea, 89
Kuek, Sherman YL, 55

LaHaye, Tim, 135
Last Supper, 132
The Late Great Planet Earth (Lindsay), 135
Latin American Pentecostalism, 24
latinization, 33
Left Behind series (LaHaye and Jenkins),
    135
Letters and Papers from Prison (Bonhoef-
    fer), 144–47
Lewis, Bernard, 97–98
libertarianism, 126
Lindsay, Hal, 135
Ling, Loun, 83
localization, and globalization, 27–28
love, commandment of, 117, 133
Luther, Martin, 146

MacArthur, John, 157
Maharishi Mahesh Yogi, 38
Mahayana Buddhist tradition, 83
Mahdism, 134–35, 139–43
manicheanism, 80
Marshall-Fratani, 68

Marx, Karl, 125
McLaren, Brian, 54–55, 152, 160–62
McWorld, 76
megachurches, postdenominational, 39
messianism, and globalization, 138–43
metaphor, 67–68
metaphysics, 67
Milestones/Signposts Along the Road/Way
    (Qutb), 127–28, 130
millenarianism, 138
missional Christianity
    about, 25, 26
    contextualization of, 50–51, 55
    in Europe, 84–93
    evangelical principle in, 58–63
    Great Commission, 47–51, 62
    indigenization, 74–75
    model of, in Paul, 63–66
    relevance of, 53–55
    Uganda Children's Project, 44–46
Modernism, 31
Montanism, 137
Moon, Sun Myung, 38
multiculturalism, 164
Müntzer, Thomas, 138
Muqtedar Khan, M. A., 128
Murray, Stuart, 26n5
mysterion, 61–64, 72, 79, 80
mystery religions, 80–84

Nasrallah, Hassan, 103
Negri, Antonio, 123–25
neo-orthodoxies, 36–37
New Age movement, 38, 161
*The Next Reformation: Why Evangelicals
    Must Embrace Postmodernity*
    (Raschke), 59n16, 152, 157
Niebuhr, H. Richard, 26, 55
Nietzsche, Friedrich, 164
nihilism, 152, 165
nirvana, 83–84

occultation, 141
Oslo Accords, 104–5

Palestine question, 100, 103–6
Paul, 63–66, 78, 154
pax Romana, 77–78

Peasants' War (Germany), 138
Peirce, Charles Sanders, 72
perspectivalism, 155
Peter, 60–62
Pharisees, 118
Plato, 117
Platonism, 71
pluralism, 74, 83, 95–96, 119, 153–55, 164
politics, 158–59
Post-Christendom (Murray), 26n5
postmodernism
    and Christianity, 25–26, 27
    critiques of, 118
    and globalization, 28–32
    participation in, 27–28
    postpomo, 151–53
    of religion, 35
prayer in schools, 57
premillenial dispensationalism, 135
preterism, 136–37
Projekt Gemeinde, 89–91
prosperity Christianity, 54
Protagoras, 155
The Pursuit of the Millenium (Cogn), 137

Qaida, al-, 36, 128
Qutb, Sayyid, 106, 107, 110–12, 127–31

Ramachandra, Vinoth, 31
Raschke, Carl, 59n16, 152, 157, 160
recursion, 40
Reformation, 79, 160
relationality, in Christianity, 117–19
relativism, 31, 153–58
Relevant magazine, 53
religion, radical and resurgent, 29–37
religious nationalism, 31
repentance, 119
reterritorialization, 28–29
rhizomic growth, 41–44, 121–27
Roe v. Wade, 57
Roman Empire, 34–35, 77–78
Romanitas, 35
Roy, Olivier, 32, 108
Rushdie, Salman, 109

Sanneh, Lamin, 42–43
Saussure, Ferdinand de, 72

Scala-Gemeinde, 85–87
Schaeffer, Francis, 152
Scopes Monkey Trial, 57
The Secret Message of Jesus (McLaren), 162
secular humanism, 152
secularization, 29–30, 32, 37, 69–70, 106
secular liberalism, 131, 149
semiotics, 28, 66–73
Shah, Timothy Samuel, 36
Silichev, D. A., 27
simulacra, 28
Smith, Jonathan Z., 79
Smith, R. Scott, 156–57
Social Justice in Islam (Qutb), 110
solidarism, 126
South, Christian, 166
Southern Baptist Convention international missions board, 74n1, 85
Soviet Union, fall of, 29–30
Spain, medieval, 95
Sufism, 102
sunyata, 84
Sweet, Leonard, 44
syncretism, religious, 69–70, 84

Tan, Kang San, 82–83, 84
taqiyya, 141
Taylor, Cooper, 88–91
tele-technoscience, 33
10/40 Window, 94

Tertullian, 137
A Thousand Plateaus (Deleuze), 121
Toft, Monica Duffy, 36
tolerance, 119, 155
Toynbee, Arnold, 33
transcendent moral collectivism, 126–27

Uganda Children's Project, 44–46
United States, 24, 37–38

Valdez, Jason, 91–92
Vattimo, Gianni, 144, 163–64
Vietnam War, 37–38
violence, and Islam, 130–31
Völkerwanderung, 124

Wagner, Peter, 39
Wahlstedt, David, 44–46
Walls, Andrew, 66
West. *See* Europe, Western
What Went Wrong? (Lewis), 97
"White Mythology" (Derrida), 67
Whose Religion is Christianity? (Sanneh), 42–43
The Will to Power (Nietzsche), 165
Wittgenstein, Ludwig, 41
Wolfe, Alan, 119
The World is Flat (Friedman), 30
Wright, Fred, 53

Zawahiri, Ayman al-, 128